China and the Future of Globalization

China and the Future of Globalization

The Political Economy of China's Rise

Grzegorz W. Kolodko

I.B. TAURIS
LONDON · NEW YORK · OXFORD · NEW DELHI · SYDNEY

I.B. TAURIS

Bloomsbury Publishing Plc

50 Bedford Square, London, WC1B 3DP, UK

1385 Broadway, New York, NY 10018, USA

BLOOMSBURY, I.B. TAURIS and the I.B. Tauris logo are trademarks of
Bloomsbury Publishing Plc

First published in Great Britain 2020

Cover design by Holly Bell

A catalogue record for this book is available from the British Library.

A catalog record for this book is available from the Library of Congress.

ISBN:	HB:	978-1-7883-1549-4
	PB:	978-1-7883-1550-0
	ePDF:	978-1-7883-1552-4
	eBook:	978-1-7883-1551-7

Typeset by Integra Software Services Pvt. Ltd.
Printed and bound in Great Britain

To find out more about our authors and books visit www.bloomsbury.com
and sign up for our newsletters.

To my Chinese friends as a heartening message.
And as a warning.

Contents

List of Diagrams		ix
List of Tables		x
List of Maps		xi
	Initial Reflections	1
1	Economy and security	5
	1. Cold War Two	5
	2. Cascade of threats	16
	3. Technology and politics	22
2	The Century of Asia with China Leading the Way?	27
	1. A country in the middle of Asia	27
	2. New Silk Road instead of exporting revolution	32
	3. Nobody likes a hard landing	41
3	People and Goods in the Changing World	55
	1. Between a demographic explosion and a population deficit	55
	2. How long, how fast?	65
	3. Where is the East, where is the West?	73
	4. Myth of the free market being perfect	83
4	Socialism, Capitalism or Chinism?	89
	1. Economy – society – state	89
	2. In search of equilibrium	99
	3. Socialism with Chinese characteristics or corrupt crony capitalism?	109
	4. Whither China and what business is it of others	124
	5. *Tertium datur*	130

5   Recipe for Crisis   133
     1. At the expense of many for the benefit of few   133
     2. Legally but immorally   137

6   What Do the Chinese Ask About?   141
     1. Right questions at the right time   141
     2. What students want to know   142
     3. Chinese panoply of questions   145

7   New Pragmatism with Chinese Characteristics   149
     1. Vision rather than illusions   149
     2. 16+1 initiative   152
     3. China coming to our rescue?   156

     Final Reflections   163

Notes   166
References   173
Index   184

Diagrams

1   Changes in major military powers' defense spending
    (percentage increase between 2007 and 2016)   7
2   US–China trade between 1985 and 2017 (in USD billions)   10
3   Wealth distribution around the world between 2010
    and 2020 (1 percent vs. 99 percent)   18
4   Doomsday Clock. How many minutes to midnight?   19
5   Share of China, India, the United States and the European
    Union in the GWP (at PPP)   43
6   Runaway China, and India trying to catch up. National
    income growth between 1980 and 2018 (GDP 1980 = 100)   45
7   Runaway China, and India trying to catch up. Per capita
    income growth (at PPP, 2011 international dollars)   46
8   Runaway China, Poland trying to catch up and Russia
    lagging behind against the backdrop of the world
    economic crisis (GDP 1989 = 100)   47
9   Population of China, India, Nigeria and the United States
    between 1950 and 2100 (in billions)   56
10 Producer's market and shortages vs. consumer's market
    and surpluses   102
11 Stagflation and shortageflation   105
12 On the other side of the looking glass, or moving from
    the inflation-shortage alternative to the inflation-
    unemployment alternative   107
13 Agricultural population in China between 1996 and 2016
    (in millions)   119
14 Changes in democracy index between 2006 and 2017   121
15 Who likes China? Percentage of people expressing a
    favorable opinion about China   157

Tables

1   The world population between 2015 and 2100 (in millions)   57
2   Proportions of private state sectors in China (percentage
    of value added, by form of ownership)   113
3   Employment in enterprises representing different forms of
    ownership in China between 1978 and 2016   117
4   Number of state-owned enterprises from selected
    countries on the *Fortune* Global 500 between 2004 and 2016   124
5   Changes in SOE presence on the list of the world's 500
    largest companies between 2004 and 2016   125
6   GDP of sixteen CEE economies in comparison to
    China (2017)   154

Maps

1 Working-age population shortages and surpluses in South
East Asia   64
2 G20 member states   79
3 Shanghai Cooperation Organization – member states,
dialog partners and observers   82
4 Eastern European countries of the 16+1 initiative   153

Initial Reflections

So what's going to happen now? And then what? What will follow next? What will be our fates? These questions are asked more and more frequently these days, 'us' standing for different entities, from individuals and various population groups, to nations and societies, to humanity as a whole; from countries and their national economies, to regions, to the entire world economy. How many times in the past have we heard that civilization was already at the crossroads, but we always managed somehow to overcome those turning points. Here we are again at the crossroads, but these look quite different to those we know from recent and more remote history.

Until not long ago it seemed that the answer to the question about the direction the world would follow depended on the degree to which the West could prove itself. Today, we can see that the West is falling well short in this regard, that it cannot properly lead the contemporary round of the battle for tomorrow as it is failing to solve fundamental civilization challenges and cannot guarantee existential rationality not only to humanity at large but even to itself. The three epoch-making challenges that need to be overcome to effectively ensure this rationality are: the population problem, the environmental issue and the income diversity syndrome. These three problems are interrelated and must be solved together. Let me put it more strongly: they will be solved together or they won't be solved at all; with disastrous consequences. In the world of the future, the power of these relations will be yet greater despite various neonationalist resentments and the old/new economic protectionism. Those specific ailments can be treated, but only if we take away the fuel that feeds them – namely, the current failure to effectively counter the mounting difficulties.

We will not solve the problems of existential rationality, which is the *sine qua non* of civilization's survival and further development, if we are not community-minded in our thoughts and actions. This is the requirement of globalization, which is irreversible for two reasons. Firstly, globalization stays with us and we stay with it for technical reasons; it cannot be abandoned due to interconnectedness of the economy, transnational financial, trade, service and manufacturing ties. Secondly, globalization will prevail because there is no economic sense in abandoning it, as this would make it impossible to solve existential economic problems. In other words, globalization cannot be escaped, for technical reasons, and there is no point in turning one's back on it, for economic reasons. That certainly does not mean that there is and will be no trouble with globalization. The trick is to use it to cope with the fundamental challenges facing civilization.

The modern times present us with a number of serious problems, which are further compounded by the fact that, during the last generation, while economic globalization made huge progress, the political one is still in its infancy. There is an interdependent, interconnected worldwide economy, but there is no entity to steer this machine. It is the height of naiveté to believe that the market can be enough here. What is needed are entities to steer the economic traffic of resources and streams, and institutions to regulate this traffic. Unfortunately, the West has shown it cannot deliver these, and, so far, nobody has stepped in to take over that role. Can it change?

It can, if there emerge powers and mechanisms capable of steering the economic processes in the long run and of implementing pro-community actions, while creatively taking advantage of the immense scientific and technical progress that luckily is here to stay. This is a huge task, but theoretically it has a solution, which must consist of reinstitutionalizing the world economy. It is necessary to couple the power of market mechanisms and the power of regulations, though the latter should be imposed with the institutional force of a global system of states, still not fully developed, rather than that of a single state. Whether this task can be successfully completed in practice will become apparent in the coming decades before civilization finds itself at yet another crossroads.

In the battle for tomorrow, nobody should be taken too lightly, but we should not overestimate anybody, either. Still, looking realistically into the future, it's hard not to recognize the growing role of China. It is, by now, the world's largest economy (if measuring production output with purchasing power), and, at the same time, a country that will have an increasing say on the way the new global institutional order is shaped. In the same way that the Chinese economy's share in global production has been growing significantly and fast in the last forty years, due to particularly high production dynamics, in the coming decades China's position in shaping this order will be growing fast and significantly, too. This is now becoming more important than how much faster production in the Middle Country is growing compared to the rich West.

For many an observer of the global political and economic scene, it is surprising how, before our eyes, China has become the champion of globalization (with its attributes such as free trade or freedom of capital flows), which would have been unthinkable merely a generation ago. This is happening because the Chinese phenomenon became possible thanks to globalization. No other country has turned it to its advantage to the extent that the Chinese have managed to do, mostly by making state-supported exports a lever for development (making great use of Keynesian instruments for that purpose, an economist will add). They can hardly be expected to oppose continued globalization, whose opponents have mostly emerged in the rich West.

This is extremely irritating to some, especially in the face of China's cultural and political distinctness from the West, which was supposed to save us but fell short of the mark. Others pin their hopes on it, seeing that China has become an economic superpower by not letting capital take control. The power remains in the hands of the state. What are its implications for the future, not only for China but also for other economies bound together by the ties of globalization? Will it be of any consequence to the world of the future or is it only some kind of Eastern happenstance?

So what's going to happen now?

Economy and Security

1. Cold War Two

The times are peaceful and yet wars are on. We are beset by a number of regional conflicts and local clashes, but they represent a lesser evil than a great global explosion. Luckily, disputes between the titans of the world have been bloodless to date. There are no saints here when it comes to intentions and acts as none of the three most powerful contemporary actors on the political and military scene – the United States, China and Russia – is free from guilt. All three are flexing their muscles, which damages international relations and reeks of a new cold war, while doing harm to economic cooperation and to efforts to create a more inclusive version of globalization.

Unfortunately, we can already speak of Cold War Two. That's how I referred to the present state of affairs several years ago, on the occasion of the 100th anniversary of the start of the First World War. Back then I wrote:

> One hundred years ago a war was unleashed. It lasted for almost four and a half years, millions of people were killed. In the beginning nobody realized it would be a world war, but it quickly turned this way. In the 1920s and 1930s, it was referred to as the Great War. It took another war, breaking out 25 years later, to get the previous one, that of 1914–1918, the name of the First World War. Soon after the Second World War, that of 1939–1945, was over, the Cold War was unleashed. This was done by the West in confrontation with the East, which was defeated decades later. It even so happened that after 1989 the 'end of history' was announced on that occasion. How prematurely …
>
> After only generation of more or less peaceful times, Cold War Two was started. Indeed, the one of 1946–1989 will be referred to by

historians as Cold War One. It was won by those who started it: the West. Now the West, too, is getting Cold War Two started. But it won't win this one. Neither will the East win it. It will be won by China, which is doing its own thing, most of all consistently reforming and developing the economy, whose international position is strengthening with every year that passes. A few years, or over a decade from now, when both US hawks with their allies, and those from Russia, get weary of their cold war imprudence, China will be a yet greater superpower; both in absolute terms and relatively, compared to the USA, European Union, Russia... Also the position of other countries, including the emancipating economies refusing to be dragged into another cold war turmoil, will be relatively better. (Kolodko 2014d)

Well, that is exactly the goal: not to get dragged into it.

The richest country in the world, the United States, instead of increasing its aid expenditure, mindful of co-creating economic foundations for peaceful development, cuts it to free up more funds for armament. Even though the level of the latter is already very high, the US Senate is pushing for a further increase of 80 billion dollars in 2019 and 85 billion in 2020 (BBC 2018b). As at 2018, the expenditure is set at 692.1 billion dollars, which represents an exponential 18.7 percent growth compared to the previous year. At the same time, Russia is reducing its military expenditure by 9.2 percent, cutting it to 2.77 trillion rubles (42.3 billion dollars) (Bershidsky 2017; Tian *et al.*, 2017). This is surprisingly little compared to the United States, but relatively much more because while the United States earmarks 'only' 3.3 percent of its budget to defense spending, in Russia it's around 5 percent. While the country's president Vladimir Putin justifies the military spending cut with the need to increase expenditure on healthcare, education, science and culture (which should be applauded), his detractors are quick to point out that it's only a short-term political marketing gimmick applied before the presidential election to be held in the spring of 2018 (which should be rebuked).

In China, the indicator describing the ratio of military spending to national income is nearly half that of the United States and stands at 1.9 percent of gross domestic product (GDP), but is growing quickly. In absolute amounts, Chinese military spending is merely a third of US expenditure, ca. 230 billion dollars a year, but let's remember that there is also expenditure incurred which is in fact military, though it's posted as purposes other than 'defense' – for example, some research and development spending that evidently serves the army is realized in the 'science' department. Let us add that this is not unique to the Chinese; others do the same.

Hence, the Chinese military spending is still a small fraction of the US one, but it must be emphasized that while the United States, despite the recently greatly increasing outlays, is still spending less than ten years ago, China is spending nearly 120 percent more. It's little consolation that others among the countries with the world's largest military budgets have increased their spending to a much lesser degree.

Analysts in the field highlight the predominance of spending on defensive weapons and facilities in all of China's defense expenditure. One of the major tasks in this area is to develop the sector manufacturing weapons that, in the event of a conflict, would push US military power back as far as possible from Chinese shores, preferably to the most

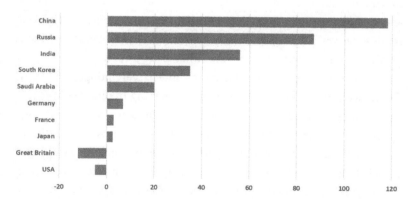

Diagram 1 Changes in major military powers' defense spending (percentage increase between 2007 and 2016)

Source: Own compilation based on data from the Stockholm International Peace Research Institute.

remote Pacific areas. So, the point is to move the enemy army back rather than deploy one's own forces closer to their shores. This strategy is known in the military jargon as *anti-access/area denial* (A2AD). This, by no means, prevents the development of various types of offensive weapons, including very sophisticated products such as drones, which China has started exporting on an increasing scale. While far behind the United States and Russia, as well as the UK and France in that respect, it is said that, with products having 75 percent capacity of the Western ones, China sells them at 50 percent of the Western price (Marcus 2018). To many buyers it's a great deal, so, sadly, the arms race is again gaining impetus.

It is all the more worrying that the US president Donald Trump, rather than looking for conciliation and creating new channels for good international and global cooperation, a year after taking the world's still most important office, announced that China and Russia are not so much the United States' partners as rivals. It comes as little surprise, then, that even such an opinion-leading weekly as the Anglo-American *The Economist* cautions against the growing threat of an eruption of conflict between the superpowers. It was no coincidence that it did so in the issue published during the annual World Economic Forum in January 2018 to further raise the adrenaline level of politicians and business people, financiers and bankers, academics and media representatives meeting in Davos (Economist 2018a). So, do we have anything to fear? And if so, who and what is the threat?

In many parts of the world, there's much scaremongering about China, its growing power supposedly threatening the peace of others. The country is feared not only by some from the same region, not only by the immediate neighbors such as Japan or South Korea, India or Pakistan, but also in more remote parts of the world, including the West, especially the United States and some European countries succumbing to Sinophobia. In others, on the contrary, China's expansion inspires some hope for a more balanced world, a new global order where a counterbalance emerges to the dominance of the West, with its eyes fixed on its own interests only.

The anti-Chinese narrative is growing stronger, in particular, among the US establishment and some, notably conservative, media and parts of the social science community. Excessive irritability is certainly undesirable and harmful in the business sphere, though it can be justified in situations where capitalists and company executives get frustrated by their inability to keep up with foreign competition, which is often identified with China. It's even worse if the ones losing their temper are politicians and lobbyists, as well as those linked to the media and the academic and research community.

What strikes me as something the world hasn't seen for a long time, maybe since the last cold war, is the aggressive, more emotional than rational public attack (rather than cold matter-of-fact criticism) of *The Economist* weekly, which entitled its cover story 'How the West Got China Wrong'. It argues that the West,

> Bet that China would head towards democracy and the market economy. The gamble has failed. … China is not a market economy and, on its present course, never will be. Instead, it increasingly controls business as an arm of state power. It sees a vast range of industries as strategic. Its 'Made in China 2025' plan, for instance, sets out to use subsidies and protection to create world leaders in ten industries, including aviation, tech and energy, which together cover nearly 40 percent of its manufacturing. (Economist 2018d)

Well, it's a fact that China, rather than adopting the path of Western-style deregulated market economy, follows that of active economic interference, by running a well-oriented industrial policy, which, mind you, many Western countries used to have in place, and some of them, for example South Korea, are still far from despising. If things were indeed as bad as persistently argued by those who are uncomfortable with the Chinese path because it makes life easier for the Chinese rather than for them, further considerations should be limited to searching for the answer to the question why this happened and what the implications are. However, the reality is far more complicated.

Of course, the criticism of China is by no means unwarranted as its economic policy and systemic solutions oriented to improving the internal situation can be costly for others, who, under the current circumstances, are unable to compete. Irrespective of the structural inability to equilibrate the US trade balance, which has been a major cause for anti-China resentments for some time now, there are also cases of China's espionage activities in the United States and other Western countries, as well as various attempts to use soft measures to influence what goes on there. However, the Chinese could learn more about this from the Americans than vice versa.

The US trade deficit is, first and foremost, the result of the country's weak and relatively uncompetive export offering rather than unfair Chinese competition, as Donald Trump and other Sinophobes would have it. The time has come to understand that the fundamental cause of the uncompetitiveness of some US sectors is living beyond one's means, which is manifested, among other things, by excessive wages, compensations and profits. In an extended cost/benefit analysis, wages emerge as the main factor determining costs, which ultimately turn out to be relatively too high on the liberalized world market. However, having recourse to protectionist practices will not be of much use in the

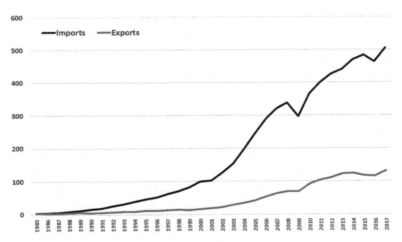

Diagram 2 US–China trade between 1985 and 2017 (in USD billions)
Source: Data from the International Monetary Fund.

long run, and a verbal attack on China will be of no use at all. It only ruins the atmosphere, which is already far from great.

When denouncing the truly immense surplus of Chinese exports to the United States over US ones to China, the countries' bilateral relations are not given a comprehensive evaluation. Compared to its national income, for instance, Poland has a relatively much higher deficit in its trade with China but is able to balance this in total foreign trade, recording surpluses in other relations. Statistics tend to simplify the reality. It's a fact that in bilateral trade relations there are twelve times fewer dollars paid to Poland by China for its direct exports going there than for imports from China. At the same time, cars, whose components are manufactured in Poland, are a substantial portion of German exports to China. Cars are the top-ranking item in the vast German exports, amounting to 1.4 trillion dollars, 6.4 percent of which go to China. Assuming that those German car exports contain, in terms of value, 10 percent of the Polish automotive industry's products, the total amount is 30–35 billion zlotys (ca. 1.5 percent of GDP). Hence, if we conduct a comprehensive analysis, it turns out that the trade exchange with China creates a lot more jobs, income and budgetary revenues in Poland than it would seem on the surface of things.

The United States is unable to do that and constantly has a major trade deficit. In 2017, it amounted to 375 billion dollars in goods traded with China, with a total gap of 566 billion dollars. This fans the flames of rhetoric targeting China and some other countries, especially neighboring Mexico, but it's still a far cry from the anti-Soviet aberration of the fevered McCarthy period of the 1950s. However, it's a fact that in Washington DC scaremongering about China is rife. 'Chinese efforts to exert covert influence over the West are as concerning as Russian subversion,' says Mike Pompeo, then head of the US intelligence, CIA. 'Think about the scale of the two economies... The Chinese have a much bigger footprint upon which to execute that mission than the Russians do' (BBC 2018a). It has to make us wonder, if not worry, when this comes from one of Washington's most influential politicians.

Quite contradictory pictures are being painted on the historic scale. In the first, imperialism – namely, the Western, capitalist variety – is supposed to be replaced with another, the Eastern and 'communist' version. Is this a real perspective or an ultimate irrationality (because neither is there communism in China, nor is the country striving to dominate the world)? In the second portrayal, China is presumed to save the world from the rampant economic and environmental dangers as it has the exceptional capacity for a long-term and comprehensive approach to problem-solving and is not selfishly focused on its interests only. The walls of our shared global house could be adorned with many more paintings that we could contemplate, as in a gallery of eclectic arts.

Contrasting values, conflicts of interest, ambiguous situations, unclear intentions cause the same facts to be interpreted quite differently. While not a word of criticism was breathed on the occasion of Angela Merkel being appointed chancellor of Germany for a fourth term in office, there was quite an uproar when the provision of the Chinese constitution limiting the presidency to two terms was scrapped. Passing over the fact that the key position in the Chinese political hierarchy is the chairperson of the ruling single party, with the president having actually little say, some are inclined to decide, for this reason alone, that from that moment on the current leader of China, Xi Jinping, becomes a lifelong dictator. Meanwhile, others emphasize that it's the right move, which, in itself, does not determine who exactly will be wielding power, but, if necessary, enables continuity in the sphere of long-term development policy leadership. And that's of crucial importance at a time when an increasing number of problems require a long-term approach.

While leaving the 'dictator or strategist' antinomy unresolved (and ignoring that, theoretically, one can be both), it's worth emphasizing that sometimes the limit on terms in office of public officials, who are elected too often for too little time, is precisely what entails short-term thinking and actions, and the obvious negative consequences with respect to socio-economic development. This kind of short-termism, or shortened time horizon in which various alternative action scenarios are considered, surely is not characteristic of the Chinese policy; quite the opposite. Many a time this is what makes the Chinese way of steering the economy superior, because the negative impact of political cycles on the economy, so typical of Western liberal democracy, does not occur in China.

In this beautiful democratic world of ours, all kinds of referendums or elections keep taking place – in Greece or Italy, in the UK or in France, in Austria or the Netherlands, in Spain or Germany – whereas all is quiet in China... Somewhere in faraway Brazil, the president was impeached, somewhere closer, in South Korea, the president was also deposed, and in the South African Republic the president was forced to resign, whereas all is quiet in China... In North Africa and in the Middle East, the Arab Spring compromised itself, whereas all is quiet in China... Even in the supposedly institutionally mature and economically advanced European Union (EU), every now and then someone needs to be rebuked or removed from the position, whereas all is quiet in China... Well, at least relatively quiet.

China, with its specific economic and political system developed over the last seventy years, has become the focus of attention of many other catching-up countries. In a situation where classical development economics failed, and fail it did (Easterly 2002, 2006), to many an economist and politician – from Bangladesh to Senegal and Ecuador, from Asia to Africa and Latin America – the Chinese model that has proven itself in practice is worth an in-depth and critical observation, as well as creative adaptation and application back home. China is a unique state, which, in just two generations (from 1978, when the gradual market reforms started) is changing its status from that of a *low income country* (as per World Bank terminology) to a *high income country*, which level it is estimated to reach as early as 2024 (Hofman 2018).

When pointing to four fundamental differences between highly and poorly developed countries, or, looking from a different perspective, rich and poor countries, what is emphasized is the superiority of the former in terms of capital endowment, technological advancement, educational capabilities, human capital quality and the development level of modern infrastructure. In each of those respects, China has made immense quantitative and qualitative progress. In some respects it is even ahead of rich countries, especially when it comes to investors' disposable capital and some elements of hard infrastructure. Suffice to say that three decades ago there were hardly 600 kilometers of motorways nationwide, and now this has increased a hundredfold to ca. 60,000 kilometers. While there were no high-speed trains at all, presently their network is 20,000 kilometers long (there aren't any in the United States). From this point of view, China is doing quite well and lags behind only slightly, if at all. Meanwhile, soft infrastructure is where the backwardness compared to the highly developed West is still visible.

Poor countries are poor mostly because they have not mastered the skills of administering the economy and regulating economic processes. Without those skills, the market alone is of little use; it is functional for a fair or a local market, but not for a greatly complex body that is the national economy, and the society and state operating within its framework. Whoever has seen the liveliness and indefatigable energy of people on the streets of Dhaka or Lima, or on the border of Nigeria and Benin, will undeniably acknowledge the laboriousness and enterprise of this human mass, but it's hard to see in this multitude of moving people and goods any sophisticated forms of organization, management, coordination, supervision, control. This may be enough when you trade in boxes of tomatoes or batteries for flashlights (imported from China, where else?), but not when it's about modern, highly complex, dynamic economic systems. What is needed is an advanced level of administration and mature regulation, which is in chronic shortage in the poorest countries.

Shortcomings in the sphere of market economy institutions are one of the principal reasons for the poor condition of economies (Acemoglu and Robinson 2012). What is meant here is institutions in a behavioral rather than organizational sense, or the rules of conduct and the rules of the game in the economy, both those codified in the regulations of the applicable laws in force and those rooted in the culture and customs resulting from practical experience (North 1990, 2005; Kolodko 2004).

In centrally planned economies, there was definitely no shortage of administration and regulation; there isn't any in China, either. However, those institutions were centralized and hierarchized in nature and would quite often take a cumbersome and overly bureaucratized form. Coupled with state socialism's typical tendency to favor hard industry, including the arms industry, this was conducive to mobilizing funds and accumulating the capital necessary for expansion, but the attendant high priority of production of the means of production did not favor production of the means of consumption. No wonder, then, that such superpowers as the Soviet Union (first) or China (later) were capable of organizing the production of a nuclear bomb and conquering space, but unable to ensure continued supplies of food products to their populations.

China, setting the historical course for catching up with developed countries, radically diminished four of the differences setting it apart from rich economies and made great progress in eliminating the institutional gap. This is achieved not only by actively adapting the institutions that prove effective in market economies of the West and modifying some of the earlier used methods of administration and regulation, but also by implementing its own original institutional solutions. Also, here one can clearly see the importance of creative continuity and change management in economy reinstitutionalization. There is still much to be done and, certainly, when it comes to catching up with rich countries in the future, there is more to be done in this very field than in the sphere of physical and human capital accumulation, modern technologies and hard infrastructure. That's where one of the main chapters of the battle for the future will play out.

But ... there is no shortage of 'buts', in the same way as there may be too little or too much cholesterol in the blood circulating in a biological organism, in a social economic circulation, too – with respect to production and storage, distribution and sale, savings and investments, banking and finance, enterprises and state – there may be too few or too many institutions. Moreover, just as there is good and bad cholesterol, there are also good and bad institutions. Thus, not every institutional change promotes growth and economic equilibrium, or contributes to economic development. Sometimes it's the opposite. If administration, intervention and regulation do not serve to accumulate capital and optimize its allocation, but serve to help bureaucratized and corrupt state apparatus – those notorious 'officials' and 'political elites', who suck out some fruits of collective economic activities – then it's akin to bad cholesterol. An organism can also suffer when there is a deficiency of good cholesterol, or when there's a deviation in the opposite direction. This happens if the weakness of the state and its regulatory functions allows unscrupulous business people, the infamous 'capitalists', to prey on the results of somebody else's work.

In contemporary China, such institutional risk is abundant as many issues are not yet finally settled, if, at all, they could be ever decided for good. Considering the economic system is *in statu nascendi* and undergoing many changes in the sphere of economic regulation, which in many cases can cause overregulation, on the one hand, and underregulation, on the other, it's hard to say which of the two currently poses a greater threat in China. Both should be constantly watched out for.

2. Cascade of threats

Today, optimism is in deficit when it comes to our outlook on the situation in the world and its evolution. Admittedly, quite enthusiastic opinions about the state of affairs can also be found. They are followed by serene expectations for the future and announcements that the situation will keep changing for the better (Ridley 2010; Pinker 2018), but they don't have enough clout. Maybe it's because pessimism comes from ongoing observation and from the attendant public narrative, while optimism comes from comparing the achievements of civilization in the long run, which are indeed impressive in retrospect.

It's a fact that human beings live, on average, a whole twenty years longer than half a century ago: 72 years now and 52 in 1960 (let's emphasize here the huge contribution of China, where this age soared from 44 to 76). Hence, no wonder there are more than two and a half times more of us (7.6 billion) on Earth than back then (3 billion). We are better nourished and clothed, we live in better-equipped and more comfortable houses, we are healthier and better educated, we know much more about one another, some of us have seen more in a year than our ancestors witnessed throughout their entire life. It's true that the population living in extreme poverty has reduced by a billion and a quarter compared to twenty-five years ago (let's emphasize, again, China's contribution). It's a fact that in 2018, the number of nuclear warheads had been reduced by as much as 85 percent compared to times where, during Cold War One, China's arsenal was the largest. It's true that currently two-thirds of humanity live in states that are more or less democratic, while two centuries ago this could be said about no more than 1 percent. Nobody in their right mind will deny that the past several generations have seen unprecedented progress, which continues today, but it does not mean that there are fewer problems or that the situation is safer. This is by no means true.

Considerable threats are piling up with respect to political tensions and military risk, especially around North Korea and in the Middle East. In the latter region, imprudent policy is aggravating already tense relations, for example when the president of the United States announced moving the US embassy to Jerusalem, outraging not only Palestinians living in this city, or threatened to break the nuclear deal with Iran, negotiated with so much effort in 2015, along with China, Russia, the UK and France – permanent members of the UN Security Council – and Germany. The same US president pulled the United States from the historic Paris climate accord on measures to protect humanity against global warming, though all other countries of the world had signed it.

Disputes continue over Russia's policies, especially in relation to the Ukrainian conflict, contributing to tensions also in parts of Eastern Europe. Despite the demise of ISIS in Syria and Iraq, we're still far from defeating terrorism, so far that the end is not in sight. Today, more or less one out of thirty people lives outside his or her country of birth as mass migration, most often poorly or not controlled at all, is not weakening or, quite the contrary, is escalating in some regions. Against this backdrop, various versions of new nationalism are emerging (Economist 2016).

Further to the unbridled greed and nonchalance of the wealthy of this transforming world, and to the insufficient activity of socio-economic policy, income and wealth inequalities keep growing (Kolodko 1999a; Piketty 2014). The immense disproportions in this field cannot be explained by absolving the economic policy and shifting the responsibility for the status quo onto the current phase of globalization or onto the nature of technological progress, which rewards more educated employees, because the true culprit here is neoliberalism, with its ideology and intentional policy of enriching few at the expense of many (Milanovic 2016). In 2017, the wealth of the poorer half of

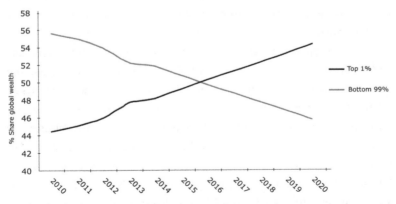

Diagram 3 Wealth distribution around the world between 2010 and 2020 (1 percent vs. 99 percent)

Source: Oxfam.

humanity did not increase at all, while the wealthiest 1 percent got hold of as much as 82 percent (*sic!*) of its growth (Oxfam 2018). It is estimated that starting from 2015, 1 percent of the richest people have had in their hands more than half of the wealth of the entire population of the globe (Oxfam 2017). Income and wealth inequalities continue to rise, which adds fuel to the already burning fire and contributes to spreading dissatisfaction with income relations in both poor and rich countries.

Hence, causes for concern are aplenty. Some believe that for those reasons the world is more unsafe now than it has ever been since the end of the Second World War. At the beginning of 2018, as it was the year before, the time remaining till the annihilation of the civilization we have been building for millennia was moved forward thirty seconds, and now the clock shows a very late time: two minutes to midnight (Bulletin 2018). That's how little time is left until doom may be brought upon man by man. This very serious warning has been communicated in this original way, since 1947, by a circle of prominent

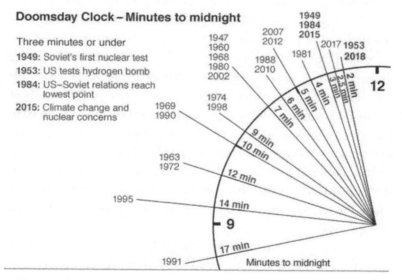

Diagram 4 Doomsday Clock. How many minutes to midnight?
Source: *Bulletin of the Atomic Sciences,* January 2018.

scholars, notably physicists, including Nobel Prize winners. Things were best in 1991, when the post-socialist transformation, launched also by Poland, was picking up speed and the Cold War, the first one, was dying out. Back then there were seventeen minutes left until midnight. Things are at their worst now …

When the previous cold war was consigned to the dustbin of history, a new one was born; one waged mostly, though not exclusively, on the economic front. Worse yet, the cold trade war is turning into a hot one (only a trade war so far and let's hope it stays that way), as the discreet and quiet disputes are being replaced by an open and loud confrontation. This is mainly happening because the West is afraid of the growing competition from the East and, more and more often, cannot keep up with it when playing fair. This does not at all mean that the East is the perfect knight and always plays by the rules; far from it. Geopolitics intermingle with geoeconomics.

The scale of hypocrisy – for the United States best illustrated by the 'do what we tell you, not what we do' slogan – is on the rise. Sheer self-righteousness. Talking constantly of free trade and the liberal economy, of technology transfer and direct investment, while resorting to protectionist maneuvers, whether openly or hidden behind political rhetoric. Meanwhile, Donald Trump talks differently, as he understands free trade as an exchange that serves the US interest, while not necessarily caring about foreign partners' interests. Admittedly, at the World Economic Forum in Davos in January 2018, he attempted to reinterpret his slogan 'America First!' as meaning not so much separately but together with others, though always adding that trade should be *fair* (that is, favorable to the United States – the way Trump understands this favorability). Unfortunately, he understands it inappropriately, for which the US economy will have to pay a high price in the long run (Phelps 2018).

This is already dangerous when Trump declares that 'trade wars are good' (BBC 2018c) and introduces a 25 percent tariff on steel imports and 10 percent on aluminum, threatening that if trade partners respond with protectionist moves (and how else would they respond, if it's a 'war'?) he will also impose a high import duty on cars – unless, that is, we treat the US president's words as eccentric excesses, but we shouldn't as this is, after all, the leader of a country which is still the world's greatest power. The United States imports four times more steel than it exports. The list of 110 countries and territories from where it takes steel products is topped by Brazil, Canada, South Korea, Mexico and Russia. China used to rank only eleventh, but in early 2018 it clearly moved up and was the main target of criticism by Trump, who announced putting in place serious protectionist instruments. While he's at it, he promotes some boorish views on Twitter, which ill become a head of state: 'When we are down $100 billion with a certain country and they get cute, don't trade anymore – we win big. It's easy.'[1]

It is, indeed, easy to say something one hasn't thought through properly, but winning a trade war is not easy, if it's possible at all. It wasn't difficult, either, to send, the next day, another original thought into virtual space about how dumb, compared to the current resident of the White House, his predecessors were: 'The United States has an $800 Billion Dollar Yearly Trade Deficit because of our "very stupid" trade deals and policies. Our jobs and wealth are being given to other countries that have taken advantage of us for years. They laugh at what fools our leaders have been. No more.'[2]

It cannot come as a surprise – or actually it should come as a great surprise if it was otherwise – that, on the one hand, in response to such words and actions, the EU and China say they don't want a trade war with the United States, but if their economies are affected, they will not stand idle, and, on the other hand, the US plans are condemned by organizations such as the World Trade Organization (WTO) and the International Monetary Fund (IMF), which points out that protectionism only appears to further US economic interests while in fact it will bring harmful results. The latter is all the more interesting, considering that the IMF is still dominated by US influence. This also goes to show how opinions on this matter are divided within the US administration and its technocratic power base.

3. Technology and politics

There's a never-ending babble about supporting scientific and technological progress and about the need to invest in energy from renewable sources. However, when this is undertaken by Sany Group Co., a Chinese private company that has cutting-edge technology and is closer than any US company to reaching grid parity, or a point where the cost of energy from renewable resources is the same as that obtained from the traditional burning of fossil fuel, the former (otherwise reasonable) US president, influenced by domestic pressure groups, blocks a wind farm project on the West Coast in the state of Oregon. Supposedly, it's too close to the port where navy ships are moored. A decision like that hasn't happened for over twenty years, when a similar protectionist instrument was used by President George W. Bush (Senior). Undoubtedly, President Obama's decision was a pre-election gesture in response to overwhelming pressure from the Republican 2012 White House contender Mitt Romney, who was more or less openly calling for an economic war on foreign countries that know how to manufacture cheaper products, especially China. This particular situation is a classic case of shooting yourself in the foot as the wind turbines were to be both designed and built on a property owned by the US company Ralls Corp. by other companies operating in the United States.

Just as in the case of protectionist tariffs for imported steel and aluminum, President Donald Trump used the contrived national security threat argument, blocking Broadcom's acquisition of Qualcomm. In reality, it's about US suspicions that Broadcom, a Singapore-based telecom company, is backed by China, and the goal is to hinder market access for China, especially for Huawei, another key industry player. Broadcom's 140 billion dollar acquisition of the US leading microchip maker could put China at the global forefront of 5G wireless technology development. So, once again, it is not about security, but about suppressing competition. It is for the same reason that Huawei was unable to conclude a contract with a US intermediary, AT&T, to sell its new smartphone model, and the Chinese company

Ant Financial, the operator of electronic payments for the leading online shopping platform Alibaba, saw its plans to buy money transfer provider Moneygram for 1.2 billion dollars blocked (BBC 2018e).

There is a major threat of more such protectionist practices adding heat to the cold economic war. Unquestionably, apart from pressure from the specific stages of political cycles (before an election, one needs to look tough and cannot let a foreign country 'spoil' the market), a major role is played by the psychosis of the unstoppable assault of the East, deliberately whipped up by the media. It is best exemplified by China, which, therefore, will be 'taken to task' most often. It is already happening on an increasing scale, sometimes beyond the limits of common sense. Where emotions take the upper hand, sound judgment is lacking.

The Committee on Intelligence at the US Congress, dominated by the Republicans who promote free market ideas, suggested completely blocking access to the US economy for two large Chinese telecom companies: Huawei Technologies and ZTE Corporation. For what reasons? Security threat: being Chinese, even though these are private companies, they must have some obscure ties to the government and army. The committee's report says that 'China has the means, opportunities and motive to use telecommunications companies for malicious purposes'. And that's why it recommends that none of the US governmental and public agencies should use Huawei and ZTE components, but also that any acquisitions, takeovers and mergers of any companies where they have a shareholding should be banned. Canada has also undertaken some restrictive measures against Huawei, under US pressure, no doubt. And yet, the United States and other superpowers from the West also 'have the means, opportunities and motive to use telecommunications companies for malicious purposes'. Is that a reason for us to block Dell, Apple or Motorola? And why not block public access to Google, Facebook or Amazon, following the example of North Korea?[3]

What is it all about? Are the Chinese companies really a threat to US interests or even to the US concern for the world peace? Maybe I should, too, disconnect the Huawei mobile device from my laptop or else, during one of my trips, the Chinese will steal the draft of this book and it will be published in their country before it appears in the United States? Let's not get paranoid! We should watch out for the Chinese but, even more so, we should watch out to keep the good sense.

The problem is that these two huge Chinese companies have become leading global firms and other corporations, including US companies, are falling behind the competition. Huawei, operating in nearly 170 countries, is the world's second largest and ZTE the fourth largest manufacturer of routers, switches and other telecoms devices. In the category of global wireless telephony companies, ZTE ranks fourth and Huawei sixth. And this is not welcome and should not continue. But it does continue, as such are the rules of technical progress in the liberalized global economy.

Some may not like the fact that the highly advocated economic freedom brings such results that the Chinese computer company Lenovo became, in the fall of 2012, the world's largest PC manufacturer, surpassing the sales of the US-based Hewlett-Packard. However, if we follow the rules of business reliability, it's only appropriate to humbly accept this and compete fairly, unless the beautiful slogans of the liberal economy are only good as long as they serve the power that be. In that case, they are nothing more than a smokescreen that allows them to keep getting rich unscrupulously. When the economic freedom, especially free trade, instead of facilitating the expansion of rich countries, investors and companies, gets them into difficulties, the principal foundations and supreme values turn out to be empty slogans.

Therefore, it's good that there's a rule of law in the most advanced countries – not always, not everywhere and not in all cases, but it's there nevertheless – rather than the rule of special interest groups. While not underestimating their influence, it is quite reassuring to see cases such as the one where the US Court of Appeals overturned the administrative ban on selling the Galaxy Nexus smartphone by the Korean giant Samsung in the United States.

After all, that was what people wanted: economic freedom, an open market, liberal trade, fair competition. If some Chinese companies are supported by government in their global expansion (and many of them are as China has not renounced the use of public aid, unlike the EU), there are better ways to compete with them than using politically motivated orders and bans, like other countries do. Mostly, bilateral negotiations serve that purpose, and if they fail, there are also the arbitration mechanisms used in the WTO practice. Most of all, however, we need to be competitive in terms of production quality. These are more effective methods of competition than unilateral sanctions as they are as much an instrument of an anti-development protectionism as a factor provoking retaliatory actions.

All we can do is count on Americans to reconsider in time, and on the Chinese not to lose their temper and not to be provoked. The United States managed in the past to win a political cold war against the Soviet Union, but will it fare well in an economic cold war against China, a country with a growing number of global companies that meet the highest technological and managerial standards, and backed by over 1.39 billion people and currency reserves worth over 3.2 billion dollars?[4]

The US reactions to the growing competitiveness and expansive momentum of Chinese high-tech companies may strike some as a sign of oversensitivity. It's not as bad as all that because only 18 percent of production is exported. The market value of Chinese technology companies amounts to 32 percent of the value of US companies. Likewise, the capital expenditure of that sector stands at 30 percent of the US level. Should one-third be referred to as 'only' or 'as much as'? I'd say 'as much as' because the relative position of Chinese companies is growing fast. When using the metric specifically designed for comparing those two giants, it is estimated that Chinese high-tech industries are at the level of 42 percent of the US industries, but they are bridging this gap very fast, as in 2012 it was merely 15 percent (Economist 2018c).

Let's not delude ourselves. In the age of globalization and its inherent battle over influence and position, there are no innocent policies and politics. China uses both spies and industrial intelligence and steals other people's ideas without patents. Yet, Americans do it, too. And also the Russians, the British, the Germans, the French and the Japanese. And the Polish too, if they only knew how and had the funds as obviously it costs money (but it pays off, too). And even if we don't approve of such practices, we must acknowledge they exist.

The Century of Asia with China Leading the Way?

1. A country in the middle of Asia

For centuries China has been known as so-called Middle Country. If it's not the middle of the world as a whole, then it's at least the middle of Asia, where increasingly developed economies and increasingly well-educated societies are gaining an increasing importance. So the question is: it is not so much China as China-led Asia that's headed for world domination? Some believe that is precisely the case and even if it's not a conscious intention of the ruling elites there, such is the logic of the historical process. In line with this interpretation, there are only 90–100 years left until the domination of the West comes to an end and its position is taken over by the East. This is predicted to happen early in the twenty-second century (Morris 2010). Well, let's wait and see, but first it's worth looking at what can already be seen …

Asia as the emerging power is much more than China. Production volume and population size are growing fast. In total, the continent is inhabited by nearly 4.5 billion people, representing ca. 60 percent of the whole planet's population, 55 percent of which is outside the Middle East, often treated separately for geopolitical reasons.[1] This human mass generates slightly over 47.3 percent of gross world product (GWP), slightly more than Europe and North America put together. From a different perspective, this is as much as eight percentage points more than the United States and the EU combined. In the future, the share of both Asian population and production will keep increasing as the population and economic growth are higher than the global rate.

It is worth realizing that once before – or actually throughout every century of the last millennium until around 1820, when the West took off with a bang as a result of the Industrial Revolution – Asia used to produce over 60 percent of the global output. In 1950, this was less than 20 percent, but it took merely two generations for this index to more than double.

Two hundred years ago – before the industrial revolution gathered momentum in England and soon after in Western Europe, and before the Middle Country turned its back to the world to stew in its own juice – China alone used to produce nearly a third of global production. It took only five or six generations of disastrous internal policy and unfavorable external circumstances, including British and Japanese colonial practices, to see this indicator tumble down, to below 5 percent half a century ago. No wonder then that some authors write about China returning to the global scene, because it's been here before.

Let me digress here. My long-standing efforts to avoid tautologies such as 'globalized world' don't seem very productive. How often is this error repeated both in common parlance and in scientific literature! The world is worldly by definition, and the globe is global, so the world cannot become worldly (or worldwide), and the globe cannot become globalized because that's the way they always are. Things that become globalized include economy, trade, capital flows, technology transfer, as well as workforce, although with significant limitations resulting from cultural, social and political reasons, and beyond the strictly economic sphere, also such wonderful things as culture and such wretched ones as terrorism. Globalization is a historic and spontaneous process of liberalization and the attendant integration of national economies and local commodity markets, which, until now, have functioned largely separately, into one big, united, interlinked and interconnected worldwide or global capital, commodity and workforce market (Kolodko 2002). Globalization also has its microeconomic aspect related to production and exchange networking through including in the manufacturing and distribution process companies from many countries that are still treated as national economies, though the economic process is increasingly supranational in nature.

The Asian continent is culturally, politically and economically very diverse, especially if we take it literally, in geographic terms, and trace its borders from Turkey and Israel in the West to Japan and Russian Siberia, with Kamchatka and Chukotka in the Far East. Leaving aside the Asian part of Russia, which usually isn't taken into account in Asian calculations, its four main cores are China and Japan as well as two regional integration blocs: ASEAN in South East Asia,[2] with no dominant economy, and SAARC in South Asia,[3] dominated by India, a regional superpower in terms of population (1.28 billion inhabitants), as well as economic (7.5 percent of global production at purchasing power parity [PPP]) and military (army expenditure representing 2.5 percent of GDP) strength.

Of the twelve countries with a population of over a hundred million, as many as seven – China, India, Indonesia (261 million), Pakistan (206), Bangladesh (159), Japan (126) and the Philippines (105) – are situated in Asia.[4] We omit Eurasian Russia, inhabited by 142 million people, of which only a quarter live in its Asian part. Soon Vietnam (population of 97 million in 2018) will join their ranks. It's worth adding that in this group of countries, Japan's population is the only one declining; every year, there are fewer inhabitants and, at the same time, they get older and older. The median age is as high as 47.3 years old, meaning that half of the population is above that age. In contrast, the societies are much younger in India (median age of 27.9) and Bangladesh (26.7). These are very important comparisons because old societies are deprived of the so-called demographic dividend, which has a negative effect on the supply of workforce in the labor market. For this reason, *ceteris paribus*, a faster economic growth can be expected in India than in China in future.

Of the twenty economies that produce more than 1 percent of global production, nine – China, India, Japan, Indonesia, Turkey, South Korea, Saudi Arabia, Iran and Thailand – are in Asia. Therefore, when reflecting on the future role of Asia, its demographic potential and culture, political significance and especially its economic influence, we need to remember that it's the world's largest region, almost in every respect.

Is it really already so bad (in the West) and so good (in the East) that Americans have to resort to unfair protectionist practices to save their skin? Or maybe the Chinese are indeed plotting to use globalization to gain control over the world? Is the era of Asian dominance really coming, with the Euro-Atlantic civilization doomed to be pushed into the background? Should we learn Chinese before we learn English? Maybe I showed a good sense of timing, not only by giving lectures at universities in Beijing and advising at the Center for China and Globalization but also by maintaining a profile on a Chinese social utility Weibo and writing the column 'Kolodko Observer' in *China Economic Weekly*?

It is beyond any doubt that China's absolute position – economically and, consequently, as is always the case for a large country, politically and militarily – as well as its impact on what is going on in the world are growing, and will continue to grow, in the foreseeable future. This process cannot be stopped, or even less so reversed, using peaceful methods, and other methods are out of the question. Everybody else must acknowledge this, regardless of their own interests and subjective affinities. Most certainly, China itself will not turn its back to the world, locking itself in disastrous autarchy, the way it did once.[5]

A country's size has its advantages, but it is also a curse. Norway or New Zealand, Canada or Australia, Chile or Malaysia, Tunisia or Bulgaria don't have to be preoccupied with staying in power as they are in no danger of gaining it. Their mission is to maintain or create welfare for their citizens, and this is enough. Meanwhile, China – the same as the United States and Russia, and, to a lesser degree, also India and Japan or France and the UK, and regionally also Brazil and Nigeria – must be strong in economic, political and military terms alike. A pacifist orientation is a luxury Singapore or Costa Rica can afford, but not China or the United States.

We need to take a leap forward again, try to make pacts with others and find the right place for ourselves in the changing world. This should be easier as currently we can clearly identify certain processes running in the opposite direction to those that occurred before. On the one hand, China, while constantly attracting the production of Western corporations, which transfer high technologies in the process, is placing more and more of its own production abroad, now having advanced manufacturing technologies, too. On the other hand, direct investment from richer countries still goes to China, but also to other economies, not only Asian, with lower salaries than in China. The beneficiaries of this situation include India and Pakistan, Vietnam and Cambodia, Bangladesh and Myanmar. This process overlaps with the effects of the continuing appreciation of the Chinese currency. So for a salary of, say, 3,000 renminbi a month, you need to earmark ca. 475 dollars, in contrast to only several years ago, when, at the exchange rate of 8.2, 183 dollars were enough for the nominal salary of half that amount – 1,500 yuans. With the increase in manufacturing labor costs, which have been rising by as much as 20 percent a year, and with the currency appreciation, China is no longer as competitive as it used to be. This is the same process that was experienced in the past by Japan, Singapore, South Korea and Taiwan, and later also by Malaysia and Thailand, though on a smaller scale.[6]

Furthermore, even in the United States and in other highly advanced economies of the West, we can observe a decline in the tendency to outsource and offshore business activities. It happens in cases where low labor costs play a relatively minor role in the overall manufacturing and sales costs for a given product. It is interesting to read estimates showing that for Apple's 16GB iPad, which was selling for 499 dollars on the US market in 2010, Chinese labor costs accounted for only 8 dollars, or 1.6 percent (Kraemer, Linden and Dedrick 2011), though maybe for more, as the calculation also includes 'unidentified' labor costs, suggesting they were incurred both outside the United States and outside China. In this situation, and in light of the political pressure to stop 'exporting jobs to communist China', a manufacturer may come to the conclusion that even if it pays five times as much for the same labor but the merchandise is made entirely in United States (and there will be no more need to explain itself about outsourcing and offshoring), the product will be assembled again near San Francisco rather than near Shanghai. It will not topple down the calculation of economic costs, but it can 'straighten out' the political narrative.

2. New Silk Road instead of exporting revolution

This time the Chinese challenge is not about the (luckily) failed former attempt to export the revolution but mostly about the successful export of goods and, quite importantly, capital. This goes hand in hand with various transactions that increase China's presence all over the world. It can be seen not only in international statistics but also with the naked eye of one traveling in different lands. What you can't see right away, however, and what is of paramount importance for the future, are the far-reaching effects of the many infrastructure projects financed in return for multiyear strategic raw material supply contracts. This is particularly visible in Africa and in Latin America but still on a relatively smaller scale in Central Asia, the Middle East, Eastern Europe and, oddly enough and importantly, in Russian Siberia. In the future, this very region will undergo dramatic changes, and a major role in this area will be played by the grand program promoted as the New Silk Road. This is the popular name of the programme known by its officially named One Belt, One Road (OBOR), or, recently, more often as the Belt and Road Initiative (BRI). It's a project of major infrastructural investments to favor expansion of trade between China and its foreign partners to the west, south and north. The program provides for cooperation with scores of countries in Asia, the Middle East, North and East Africa and in Central and Eastern Europe (CEE).

What is the BRI? How should one approach it? Is it a policy or an institution? Or maybe an organization or a structure? I believe it's best to refer to it the way the Chinese themselves suggest: as an initiative. Or a project. There are always two I-words behind all projects: ideas and interests. It is also the case now, however, contrary to the era when Chairman

Mao wanted to export the communist revolution, that ideas are consigned to the background. Even though some accuse China of planning an ideological and political outward expansion, it is clearly not about persuading others to follow the Chinese path or even imposing the Chinese economic and political model, but about economic goals. Indeed, in some regions of the New Silk Road, for example in the Central Asian countries – where, incidentally, the old Silk Road used to thrive and left a mark ages ago – a political system with Chinese characteristics may seem more attractive than the Western liberal democracy, but in CEE hardly anyone is inspired by it.

Chinese politicians and economists emphasize the imperative to continue globalization, and no wonder as they gained from it more than anybody else. At the same time, they stress the need for changing the nature of the globalization process. That's why there's so much talk of 'transforming globalization', which should be inclusive and ensure equitable distribution of the fruits of supranational cooperation in all fields: from the economy and natural environment to security and technology, to science and culture. In this context, the instrumental importance of the BRI is highlighted. It is an initiative aimed to help transform globalization from its existing form, which is rejected by many, to a globalization that will be more socially useful on a global scale than the one the West used to offer. That's why some countries, more often from outside the West, pin great hopes on it, while others, within the West, express some concerns. The former are wondering what such 'globalization with Chinese characteristics' can bring them, the latter would probably rather not experience it, and yet some others are watching with interest what will come out of it ...

What definitely comes to the fore is the second I-word – interests. Big interests, as it is a big project, considering its momentum, though its scale is still not fully known, even in Beijing. The BRI is said to encompass sixty-five countries of Asia, Europe and Africa, inhabited by over 60 percent of the world's population on 38.5 percent of its area. Trade between those countries accounts for 35 percent of the world's turnover, their GDP represents 30 percent of global production, and household consumption accounts for 24 percent of what's consumed by humanity as a whole.

As emphasized by the Chinese authorities, the BRI creates great opportunities for cooperation in five areas:

- cultural exchange by promoting people-to-people bonding and cooperation;
- policy coordination by planning and promoting large infrastructure development projects;
- financial integration by strengthening monetary policy coordination and bilateral financial cooperation;
- trade and investment by promoting cross-border investment projects and cooperation in chains of supply;
- connectivity by creating facilities for contacts along the belt and road.

Even though the project name contains the word 'road', it is by no means clearly marked out by the authors. There are no official maps showing where this road should run, so the ones in use are drawn quite randomly; a cartography of sorts is developing. Of course, in countries the project intends to include, the road should run through their territories. The BRI map also features twelve African ports, ten of which lie outside Egypt, the only country from this continent to be officially included in the project. Exactly who included whom in this initiative and based on what rules?

The answer, obviously, is China, though the rules are not completely clear. It's a fascinating geopolitical and geoeconomic game, whose goals and rules are laid out only vaguely. There are many players, cards have been ostensibly dealt, but maybe not all of them yet. And it's not clear whether the game goes on only on the table, or whether some cards are being played under it. Who risks what and in the name of how high a hypothetical win? Political declarations can be accused of vagueness and, of course, are full of assurances of the initiator's good faith, but in many a place across Eurasia – and elsewhere, too – they give rise to various reflections, doubts, suspicions, concern. Economic goals are still drawn with a thick line and it's hard to form a clear opinion on what will be built, and why and when and with whose money, and how it will be managed. And that's how this open-ended game of sorts plays out.

Still, those invited to participate flock to it, reckoning that it costs nothing to join the project at this stage, and maybe it will bring some, possibly major, economic benefits with time. Reputation is also not at stake, because despite the intensifying attacks on China from the West, cooperation with the country is a self-evident fact. Therefore, nobody refused to take part in the project, even countries whose relations with the Middle Country have been recently far from perfect, such as Vietnam or the Philippines. It should be strongly emphasized that only China can afford such a huge project, announced and initiated at its sole discretion.

If the United States proposed something similar, bearing the name of, say, 'Great Americas', and pulled out a map of an area stretching from Alaska to Tierra del Fuego, the plan would fall flat, because surely several Caribbean and Latin countries, for example Haiti and Venezuela, would not obey such a dictate. If the EU announced, say, a 'Euro-African Project', without adequate *ex-ante* agreements, some of the postcolonial countries could decline to take part in such an enterprise. Proposing a project that Pakistan and India, Poland and Russia, Israel and Syria, Myanmar and Bangladesh, Saudi Arabia and Iran, Nepal and Bhutan want to join more than willingly and without any preconditions is something only China can pull off.

When you look at the map of the world, the geographic criterion is the first one to catch your attention. The project involves nearly all Asian countries, all of CEE and Egypt, because what kind of road would it be if the Suez Canal was not on it? Nearly all of Asia – because, for political reasons, the two Korean states and Japan are missing. The former, because it was impossible to sign up only South Korea, and since the North Korea has strict sanctions imposed on it, China preferred to avoid accusations of collaboration with the Pyongyang regime. The latter, because relations with rich Japan are far from good and including it in the BRI would most likely require negotiations, and there is no favorable political climate for it, sadly. What is missing at the edges of the map is, on one side, Finland and Greece, because these are Western European countries, and, on the other side, Papua New Guinea, because it's already part of 'Australia and Oceania'. Hence, due to a sort of political correctness and to simplify the presentation, the map of countries the New Silk Road is to go through on land and sea includes countries such as East Timor or Bahrain, Macedonia or Estonia, though probably no camel will ever walk that way nor will any boat sail nearby.

Essentially, China did not ask any countries whether they wished to be included in the project. First it signed up whoever was necessary – which, apart from the aforementioned exceptions, was determined by the map – and then went on to announce it. However, if a country is missing from the list, it does not mean they are left out altogether, like Greece for example. While the country, a NATO and EU member state, is not included, the port of Piraeus, largely owned by Chinese capital, is marked.[7]

Latin American states were not formally invited to the BRI but the hosts refer to the region as the 'natural extension' and 'indispensable participant' of the project. Talk is talk, but China is doing its thing, investing more and more money in Latin America and encouraging its companies to penetrate markets over there, unlike the neighbor to the north, which discourages investment, with Donald Trump's behavior offending some, including Mexico and Salvador in the process. Precisely at the time the US president, in his usual style, maintains he said something else than the actual statement he made at the World Economic Forum in Davos a year after the Chinese president gave his speech there, the Chinese foreign minister Wang Yi, at the meeting of all thirty-three member states of the Community of Latin American and Caribbean States (CELAC – Comunidad de Estados Latinoamericanos y Caribeños), speaks against trade protectionism and offers the region a 'strategy of mutual benefit and shared gain' (Economist 2018b).

In truth, so far nobody knows exactly how much, where, when and how the Chinese plan to invest when implementing the New Silk Road project, both along its land and maritime sections. However, the amount is rumored to be 4 trillion dollars, which must impress everybody, even in the richest countries situated slightly further away, at the end of the road, in France and the UK, because it's more than their GDP. No wonder that in both those countries, the arrival of a freight train from China, which had come a long way using the existing infrastructure (and signaling the need for modernization and extension, which is the main idea behind the New Silk Road), was greeted with nothing short of a celebration. The same happened in Poland when in June 2016 a freight train arriving from China was welcomed at the platform by Polish president Andrzej Duda and Chinese president Xi Jinping on his official visit to Poland. It is also no wonder that Western European politicians making official visits to Beijing in early 2018 – in January the president of France, Emmanuel Macron, a month later the prime minister of the UK, Theresa May – talked more about trade and investment than about security and international relations. Everybody wants a little share of those four trillion dollars …

In poorly developed countries, China spends a lot of money on the infrastructure to strengthen human capital: schools and universities, outpatient clinics and hospitals. Soft credit is used for that purpose, which on various occasions is partly canceled and becomes subsidies. In the process, large Chinese construction companies are often hired to carry out projects, so no wonder they become major global players. If we take a closer look at the geopolitical map of the world from this angle, it's easy to note that China is especially active where the West has failed. Once, in the colonial period, when it exploited locals instead of helping them, later, in the neocolonial era, when it cheated them instead of being cooperative, and recently, in the age of globalization, when, at times, it marginalized them instead of creating areas of positive synergies.

Curiously enough, China is also active where the Soviet Union, and especially Russia as its core, fell short of expectations. This disappointment is still casting a long shadow in Kazakhstan, Kyrgyzstan, Tajikistan, Turkmenistan and Uzbekistan on the politics and economy as well as on the culture and mentality. Geography and history are one thing, and contemporary interests are another, which can be seen especially clearly in those post-Soviet Central Asian republics. In this interesting region, where political stability and sustainable development cannot be taken for granted, we're dealing with a unique mixture of deeply rooted characteristics resulting from Russian, Asian and Islamic influence as well as from the Soviet legacy. To these, we can now add Chinese and also Western influences. The latter is due, on the one hand, to the region's growing importance in combating international terrorism, whose tentacles reach those lands, and, on the other hand, it results from the abundant energy resources, which are meaningful on the global scene.

It should be emphasized here that geographic location, which is not up to the economy and politics, can be either a blessing – the way it is for Switzerland, surrounded by Germany, France, Italy and Austria – or a curse – as experienced by Iraq, situated between Iran, Turkey and Saudi Arabia. Whether the post-Soviet Central Asian republics, which occupy a major spot on the New Silk Road, manage to put this aspect of their location to their advantage or let themselves be taken advantage of depends on the political craft and ability to pursue favorable national socio-economic development strategies. Any country that lies in a zone where China and the United States, the EU and Russia are vying for influence, may find itself at the losing end, but may also discover there is much to gain. To make it happen, though, first and foremost, one cannot get drawn into conflicts with the others or in relations with those big global players.

Although Chinese activity obviously contributes to reducing poverty and promotes social and economic development, China, also for this reason, is suspected or even accused of ill intentions, ideological indoctrination and political corruption. Even if it were partly so, this doesn't change the fact that such a strategy helps less advanced economies in their emancipation efforts. If this also poses a threat to the balance of influence, then instead of wasting time criticizing Chinese expansion, the rich West had better increase its own aid and pragmatically reorient the operating methods and policy directions of international organizations that are greatly influenced by it.

There is nothing wrong, quite the opposite, if in the process of exporting capital and goods, China also 'exports' some of its good skills in the field of soft infrastructure. These are the good practices so eagerly discussed in management science (Cieślik 2016). If in China itself even the fastest trains cannot run without proper traffic regulation, or having a larger number of well-educated personnel does not automatically ensure socio-economic progress, clearly it's even less likely to work in economies lagging behind China. Hence, they can and should learn from that country. Knowledge and skills are today an especially valuable 'commodity'. I deliberately use inverted commas as it's not about a literal commodity (i.e. a product of human work intended for market exchange), since in this case it's often a matter of non-cash transfers.

Tens of thousands of foreign students are in China on scholarships, studying at faculties preferred from the point of view of China's external expansion. When I used to give lectures at a university in Beijing to a group of forty scholarship holders, they all came from 'developing' countries, the most developed of them being Turkey and Kazakhstan. Nearly all of them – with the exception of a Polynesian from Tonga and a Caribbean from the Bahamas – are citizens of countries included in the New Silk Road, or countries, which due to their location in Africa, are the focus of the Middle Country's attention. There are no coincidences here.

China is also using its presence and growing activity in international organizations, especially in the World Bank, IMF and Asian Development Bank (ADB), to exert pressure on institutional solutions and on the development policy directions and instruments in the countries to which those organizations extend their financial aid and expert advice. The country has by no means upstaged Western influence, especially in the World Bank and IMF, but in the emancipating economies Chinese experts can be seen more and more often, delegated there by those and other international organizations, and here and there the 'Chinese spirit' can be increasingly felt.

All this is followed by a diplomatic offensive. Currently, Beijing hosts 166 embassies and has as many of its own worldwide. The United States has one more, 167. Soon, however, it will also be surpassed in this

respect the moment any of the countries that have until now considered
Taiwan as Chinese representation changes its mind. The remnants of
the Cold War period, the first one, are twenty Taiwanese embassies:
as befits an island, six of them are located in island countries of the
Pacific and five in the Caribbean, five in Central America and one in
South America, two in small African countries, and in the Vatican. A
time will come, once the People's Republic of China (PRC) and Taiwan
are reunited (and they will be), when China has the most diplomatic
representations in the world. At present, if we count all diplomatic
missions, not just embassies, China has 268, and the United States, 273.
For the sake of comparison, let me add that Russia has 242 missions
and France, 266.

For around eighty countries China is the largest or second largest trade
partner. Little wonder then, that what happens there greatly determines
what happens elsewhere in the world economy. When it comes to
Chinese exports, worth 2.2 trillion dollars, the number one market
is the United States (18.2 percent), followed by (and leaving out Hong
Kong, to which the PRC sells 13.8 percent of the goods exported) Japan
(6.1), South Korea (4.5) and Germany (slightly less). When it comes to
imports, which are ca. 425 billion dollars lower, number one is South
Korea (10.0 percent), closely followed by Japan (9.2), Germany (5.4)
and Australia (4.4). The United States ranks below all those countries,
with lower exports to China than those from Australia. Let's note –
as it's interesting – that the New Silk Road does not run through two
neighboring countries, South Korea and Japan, to which as much as
one-fifth of Chinese exports go. One of the reasons why, to a certain
extent, is that they are highly developed and have their own advanced
infrastructure.

Dependence on the Chinese economic situation can be observed
on many levels and goes far beyond direct exports and imports. In the
literature on the subject, the term 'Sinodependency index' has even
been coined, an index that reflects changes in the S&P 500[8] stock index,
which depends on the position of 135 listed companies that derive their
revenues from operations in China (Economist 2013). If the Chinese

economy is on the rise, so are the stock market prices, and vice versa. Between 2009 and 2012, the years marked by the world crisis, the Sinodependency index grew by nearly 130 percent, while the complete S&P 500 rose by slightly over 50 percent. In other words, if it weren't for the continued Chinese boom, the economy would be in a poorer condition, and so would be stock exchanges in many other countries, including the most developed ones. Therefore, whoever wishes China ill, wishes himself ill.

3. Nobody likes a hard landing

Some people wish China ill for various irrational reasons: either out of jealousy, because it's 'communist', or out of stupidity because they don't understand that they can hurt themselves in the process. Let us have a look for a moment at what would happen if Chinese growth lost its momentum or radically collapsed. At the beginning of this decade, the Chinese economy was already growing at a visibly slower pace than in the previous three decades, both due to stagnation and recession in the crisis-torn West and for internal reasons. A double-digit GDP growth, 10.8 percent, was last recorded in 2010.

It must be emphasized that, though lower than before, it is still one of the highest growth dynamics in the world and is the main driving force that keeps global production on a growth path. It's mostly thanks to China and India (in the period between 2015 and 2017, the latter recorded a 'Chinese' GDP growth, amounting in those three years to 8.0, 7.1 and 6.7 percent respectively, or 23.4 percent in total), and to some other emancipating economies, that world production rose in those years by 3.3, 3.1 and 3.5 percent respectively. Over the same period, Chinese GDP increased by over 22 percent, growing by 6.9 percent in 2015, by 6.8 in 2016 and again by 6.9 in 2017. In total, in recent years around three-quarters of the global production growth is owed to the gross production growth – more than double the global average rate – recorded in China and India; or in Chindia, as those two giants could be called jointly. These are only two out of the nearly two hundred states in the world but account for as much as 36 percent of the global population.

The significant acceleration of the economic growth rate, first in China, then in India, in one and a half generations, drastically changed the landscape of the world economy. While the two countries' joint share of GWP in 1980 was barely 5.4 percent, by 2017 it had reached 25.7 percent (*sic!*). In other words, it had risen – mainly thanks to China – nearly five times, from slightly over a twentieth of global production to a quarter. What it obviously entails, though still shocking, is that at the same time the joint share of the United States and EU dropped by as many as 20 percentage points, from 51.9 to 31.8 percent. This has its implications as such giant changes in geoeconomics must be followed by far-reaching changes in geopolitics.

The nosedive of the United States and EU's share of global production in 1992 must make us wonder. After all, there was no economic disaster; it was the Soviet Union, not the United States or the EU, that collapsed. In the highly developed part of the world, this was a relatively peaceful time in terms of politics; a year before we were the farthest, in the postwar period, from the 'midnight apocalypse' – as many as seventeen minutes away. So, where did this exponential fall in the share of global production come from – by 1.5 percentage points (from 21.4 to 19.9 percent) in the case of the United States and by as much as 2.3 percentage points (from 27.1 to 24.8 percent) for the EU? Well, not from real processes but from methodological changes in estimating PPP.

To measure it adequately is a highly complicated statistical problem, as you need to compare a representative basket of goods and services. Not only do their prices change but also some goods disappear from the basket and new ones are added. That's why, on a periodical basis, all international organizations, the World Bank and the IMF, revise PPP. Since its release in November 2017, the iPhone X has been added to the basket, so we compare the purchasing power of income by checking which part of our salary we have to spend on it in Shanghai and which part in New York. Once upon a time, this basket contained CDs with

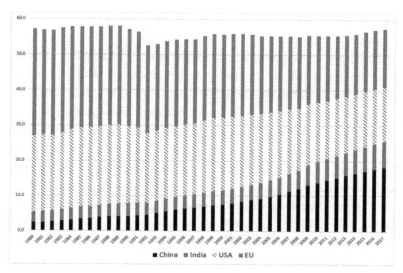

Diagram 5 Share of China, India, the United States and EU in GWP (at PPP)
Source: Own calculation based on IMF data.

our favorite music, now they can be replaced by the cost of using Spotify's services. Electricity prices and house rents, share of food or housing spending, costs of education and medical treatment, they all change. All this has major consequences for how the purchasing power of income develops.

By way of example, a Chinese professor flying to the United States for a conference can exchange there 6,300 renminbi for 1,000 dollars (leaving the commission aside) and, on average, he can purchase for that amount goods for which he would pay only around 3,250 renminbi back home. One dollar, which is worth 6.3 renminbi on the money market, has a purchasing power of ca. 3.25 renminbi.[9] Or, to put it differently, if a US professor earns 10,000 dollars, in China he could exchange it, at the market rate, for 63,000 renminbi, but in the United States, considering the US price level and structure of spending, this will only buy him what his Chinese colleague purchases in his country for merely 32,500 renminbi. China is simply cheaper, and the United States more expensive, but how much cheaper or more expensive depends on the structure of the basket of goods considered in comparisons, hence the large differences in macroeconomic accounts.

Following that adjustment, the contribution of Atlantic economic superpowers to the globe's total production was more or less stable for a decade, and then it started decreasing again, which process still continues, but let's remember that in those comparisons we are relying on metrics that are imprecise and far from perfection. It is also the methodological changes in the structure of the basket of goods used for comparisons and for verifying the market prices of goods and services contained there that account for the otherwise paradoxical case of the decline in the EU's share of global production in the period between 2003 and 2005, from 22.6 to 21.5 percent, despite eight post-socialist economies joining this grouping in the spring of 2004. Back then, they produced in total nearly 2 percent of global production, and all of a sudden the EU's share, rather than growing by 2 percentage points, drops by 1 percentage point. During the same interval, the United States' share also fell, this time by 0.6 percentage points, from 19.9 to 19.3 percent. Such a statistical view of reality most likely comes from the fact that the additional real 2 percent from CEE was 'sucked' into the nominal methodological efforts that made the analyzed indicator go in a direction opposite to the EU enlargement.[10]

These days, some are quick to point out that India has brought its growth rate closer to the Chinese dynamics. Some report this with satisfaction, but not because India has sped up, but because China has slowed down. Indeed, in the last couple of years, the GDP growth rate in those two most populous countries of the world has been similar, nearly 7 percent. Even though, with a population close to that of China, India's contribution to global production still remains less than half that of China, because it's a poor country with an annual per capita income of only 7,200 dollars (at PPP), representing 43.4 percent of the value generated by China.

This difference in the production volume translates into the standard of living being clearly higher in China than in India. A generation ago, we had two hugely populated poor countries, now we have only one. This occurred because, in the period between 1981 and 2018 (assuming that in the last year GDP growth will be at the level recorded a year before), the average growth rate in India was not at all low, 6.4 percent, but that of China was very high, as much as 9.5 percent. Consequently, in the former country, real GDP (at fixed prices) grew by slightly over ten times, whereas in the latter, it was a staggering thirty-two times. In that period the population of India increased by ca. 87 percent, while that of China rose by ca. 42 percent.[11]

It is truly astonishing that, taking account of the projections for the several years remaining to the full four decades, China has managed, in just forty years (truly a blink of an eye compared to historical processes), to increase its real per capita income around twentyfold! This is a result of an unprecedented capacity for a systemic combination of a private free market economy and state-planned economy at a time of tremendous technological progress. India took a different path and that's why it's much poorer than China, though throughout the 1980s it was still slightly richer. Or, to be more accurate, slightly less poor.

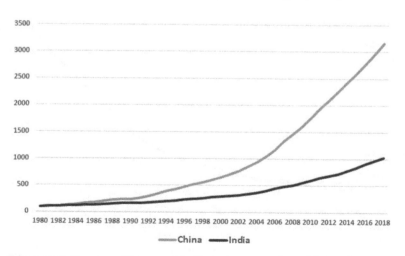

Diagram 6 Runaway China, and India trying to catch up. National income growth between 1980 and 2018 (GDP 1980 = 100)
Source: Own compilation based on IMF data. Own forecast for 2018.

Consequently, the real purchasing value of income per each of those more and more numerous people grew in this period nearly five times and twenty-two times, respectively. Against this backdrop, we can see clearly what an outright disaster – as calling it a failure would be an understatement – Russia's inept political transformation and attempt to enter into globalized economic relations is, to say nothing of the even worse case of Ukraine, but the latter, albeit a regionally important and geopolitically significant country, has no importance on the global economic map. Even Poland's case, despite all the reservations, a success story on a CEE scale (and some even say on a global scale), seems mediocre by comparison. Since 1989, the year of transformation acceleration in the countries of post-socialist Europe, GDP in China has been growing every year more than three times faster than the world economy, whereas in Poland it was growing a bit more slowly.

As a result, Poland's share of the global economy in the last thirty years has fallen rather than risen, as insufficiently astute observers

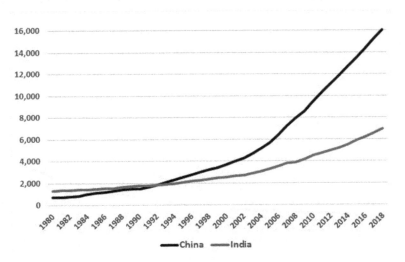

Diagram 7 Runaway China, and India trying to catch up. Per capita income growth (at PPP, 2011 international dollars)

Source: Own compilation based on IMF data.

tend to believe. Compared to its close neighbors, Poland looks splendid, but, unfortunately, not so good in comparison with many, more remote, economies.

In development economics there is a popular term, 'hard landing'. It is contrasted with 'soft landing', defined as descending gradually and softly from high production growth levels. Hard landing means an abrupt growth rate decline, just as when a plane, during the last phase of the flight, goes down at an unpleasantly sharp angle and then touches the hard ground, distressing the passengers. For economic growth, this doesn't necessarily mean going to a ground or zero level but sharply below the previous trend. During the last crisis, at the beginning of the second decade, a lot of Western countries experienced the shock caused by hard landing. This calamity particularly affected first the United States, then Spain, Greece, Ireland and Portugal, as well as basically the entire eurozone, whose economy, from a decent GDP level of 2.0 percent in 2010, went down to a recession of -0.4 percent in 2012.

For over a decade now, we have been continually hearing of the imminent 'hard landing' of the Chinese economy. As yet, however, the

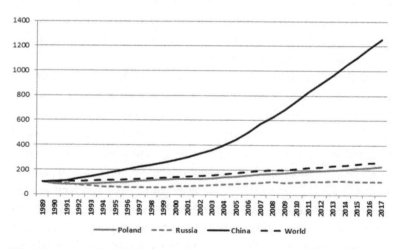

Diagram 8 Runaway China, Poland trying to catch up and Russia lagging behind against the backdrop of the world economic crisis (GDP 1989 = 100)
Source: Own compilation based on IMF data.

reality has surprised us, giving the lie to the blackest forecasts. For ten years in a row, from 2001 until 2010, GDP growth exceeded the IMF's forecasts announced at its spring summits. By the way, this is not an isolated case. Others are also wrong in their forecasts. The GDP of the four largest developing economies, the 'emerging markets' – Brazil, Russia, India and China – in 2008 was 75 percent higher than the eminent US investment bank Goldman Sachs had forecasted just five years earlier, when it used the term BRIC (O'Neill 2012) for the first time, a constantly overused acronym formed by the first letters of those countries' names.[12] Such a miscalculation came from clearly underestimating the growth dynamics of China, as well as that of India, another Asian colossus.

What is 'hard' and what is 'soft' is not determined in this case by mathematics or even less by physics but rather by the methodological convention. You can say that a hard landing was experienced by the Polish economy, when it descended in a short period of only two years from a high growth rate of 7.4 percent in the first quarter of 2007 to a trace level of 0.8 percent in the first quarter of 2009. What other than a 'hard landing' do we call losing as much as 6.6 percentage points of the previous production growth? This was by no means enough to stop government propaganda from hailing Poland as a sort of 'green island', as it was the only country in the EU where recession was not recorded in any quarter during the world economic crisis.

Another type of simulation was conducted for China, assuming that a 'soft landing' would mean investment growth rate in China declining by 2 percentage points, while a 'hard' one would be indicated by a drop of 3.9 (Ahuja et al. 2012). If such a hypothetical situation had occurred in 2012, of all the major trade partners, South Korea would have been the most affected. Instead of the 3.6 percent GDP growth predicted for it by the IMF, in the event of China's 'soft landing', the rate would have dropped to 2.3, and in the event of the 'hard' one, as much as three times, down to 1.2 percent. The response of two other major regional partners, Japan and Australia, would have been slightly weaker, and an even weaker, though still considerable, response would have been exhibited by Brazil (instead of a 3 percent growth, 2.8 and 2.6 respectively in each variant) and Germany (instead of 0.6 percent, 0,4 and 0.2 respectively). All this with the investment level reduced by only 2 or nearly 4 percentage points. And yet accumulation and investment are much more susceptible to the growth fluctuations and changes in the absolute level than the gross product is because they are often treated as a buffer to protect against overly drastic changes in the consumption level.

Chinese capital markets aren't free from trouble, either, but who is? They are increasingly well regulated and supervised, but they are markets rather than state-owned enterprises, which is why they do not pay heed to the authorities but instead to the sentiments of investors and profiteers, mainly domestic ones, though those from abroad are growing in number. In the event of major frictions, the authorities, to prevent share prices from plummeting and to keep the economy running, resort to persuasion, encouraging domestic capital to invest on the stock exchange. This does no harm and sometimes can even help. Though the Chinese market is still far from the level of sophistication we can observe in the powerful economies of the West, it is becoming increasingly rich and mature, representing a major source of capital, thus helping to finance economic growth.

Market valuations of companies listed on the Chinese stock exchange are at present definitely more justified by their actual condition and competitiveness than they were three years ago. ChiNext – P/E (price to earning) ratio, or the share market price to earning per share of high-tech companies, treated as China's response to the American NASDAQ – at the beginning of 2018 (already after the 10 percent plunge on 9 February) stood at 42, much higher than NASDAQ, but also definitely more realistic than the rate of 150 recorded before the financial market collapse in 2015. CSI 300, the index of the largest Chinese companies, shows a P/E ratio of 14, quite decent compared to the ratio of 25 for the S&P 500, the most followed share index in the United States.

Another decade of fast growth in the Chinese economy is coming to an end and the country somehow has no intention of undergoing a hard landing; it keeps rising at a rate where the income nearly doubles in ten years.[13] Therefore, an important question presents itself: are we really in for a hard landing of the Chinese economy? And if it were to happen, what consequences would it have? What should the rest of the world, especially its rich regions in Asia, Europe and United States, wish for? Would it be good if the Chinese boom continued as it keeps the economy buoyant in other countries, or maybe it would be better if China slowed down its long march forward as it threatens the dominant position of others? Does this long-lasting Chinese prosperity contribute to balancing the global economy or does it, in fact, throw the economy off balance?

The answer is clear: the highest possible production growth rate in China is in the best interest of both the country itself and the rest of the world. Of course, there are several conditions to be met: in particular, a more environmentally friendly path must be adopted and income disparity reduced. This will contribute to the improved living conditions of hundreds of millions of people in China and provide additional growth impulses in other places in the world. It's enough to realize that every additional billion dollars of Chinese purchases in CEE means a noticeably higher employment rate in Poland, higher incomes in Ukraine and growing profits in the Czech Republic.

China's hard landing cannot be ruled out; its problems and challenges abound. In the short run, one of the main problems is the overcapacity resulting from overinvestment in earlier periods (Kobayashi 2017). This is true mostly of metallurgy and some industries that provide supplies for the construction industry. China is producing too much cement and steel, and if the existing capacity was put to nearly full use – as happened during the years of a two-digit growth rate – the country could produce even more of those commodities. The problem is there is not enough demand for them inside the country, and it's not easy to export the surplus production as China's efforts in this regard meet with resistance from countries that cannot keep up with Chinese competition.

Foreign observers of the Chinese performance on the global scene sometimes see the fast-growing stream of direct foreign investment (FDI) from China as not only economic but also political expansion, or, horror of horrors, a relaunch of imperialism, this time *à la chinoise*. Indeed, during those seven fat years – when the West was struggling with the effects of the self-inflicted crisis and reduced DFI in the process – China greatly increased its investment in other countries. So far, it has not invested widely in Central Asia, even less in CEE, but, on the other hand, very extensively in Africa. In the period between 2011 and 2017, its investment in Africa amounted to ca. 280 billion dollars, of which ca. 30 percent went into transport, with slightly less in the energy sector, followed by metals. There are three reasons for this. We know the first one already: this is a way to export some of the surplus domestic supply by processing cement and steel into reinforced concrete for infrastructure constructed on the African continent. A second reason is to build traffic routes – road, railway and maritime alike – to be used to transport more and more of the raw materials mined there, which are necessary to keep the Chinese economy running. This also includes air routes, as more and more people will be on the move as well. But there is also a third reason. So far, Africa imports relatively little from China, as the countries are poor, with not enough rich people to sustain a thriving market. This will change, however. Just think that even if, halfway into the century, only a tenth of Africa's population is wealthy, let's say with incomes at the level of today's US middle class, this will represent for China a bigger market than Europe, with its middle class. China recognizes this and is the main reason why it invests there, while also getting to help Africa in the process.

It's not hard to guess that the United States is not happy about this, though it's a shame its own economic interests in the Dark Continent are very modest, and the aid commitments embarrassingly low. It did not stop the US secretary of state, Rex Tillerson, while on a visit to several Central African countries, from criticizing China for its much greater engagement, accusing the country of having 'encouraged dependency, utilized corrupt deals and endangered [...] natural resources' of the African economies (BBC 2018d). How unconvincing those allegations are when confronting the modest half a billion dollars earmarked by the United States for additional aid for Africa, on the occasion of Tillerson's visit, with the tens of billions of dollars invested by the Chinese, especially when President Trump's reference to poor African countries as 'shithole countries' just weeks earlier is still fresh in the memory (Watkins and Phillip 2018).

In the long term, on the other hand, the most serious of the challenges are the economic and social consequences of an aging population. Half a century ago, the state system pension of every Chinese person was funded from contributions of five people of working age; at present, it is funded by only three people. Presently, there is one elderly person, no longer fit to work and earn money, per five employees; very soon, as early as 2035, there will be one such person per two employees. It's worth pausing here for a while and letting your imagination run free: a country with a population of almost one and a half billion, where two working people have by their side one person of retirement age …

Let's have our imagination work a bit more. In the 2+1 family model, when parents were not allowed by the administration to have more than one child, a vast majority of them preferred a son. Obviously, it's a self-evident discrimination against girls and women, if we stretch the time perspective far enough, but these are the facts. Controlling the gender of a child before it was born led, on a social scale, to a situation where we currently have 106 males per 100 females on average. Since the average lifespan of men in China is more than four years less than women (only 73.6 compared to 78 years), in a group of people aged over 65 there are 92 men per 100 women. This isn't a problem among the elderly; not at all, because at this age you're less likely to be looking for a spouse. At the other end of the demographic pyramid, where life starts, there are as many as 114 boys per 100 girls. When the former look around for the latter, which happens especially in the 15–24 age bracket, insurmountable difficulties emerge. Assuming that all of them want to get married and start a family and that none of the women stays single, as many as fourteen men won't find a wife. This is an additional factor that frustrates many Chinese, which would not be solved even if polygamy were to be introduced. Such gender disproportions will continue for a long time, making it difficult to develop social harmony. Ownership relations may be acceptable, but maybe the lack of fiancé candidates will trigger a social revolt?

People and Goods in the Changing World

1. Between a demographic explosion and a population deficit

The United Nations (UN) expects, in its population forecasts, that a demographic peak may occur in China as early as 2026. This marks a point after which the population will first temporarily stabilize and then start falling. Importantly, population numbers will be, at the same time, growing fast elsewhere, including countries that are already populous today. This is true of India, where the demographic peak is expected in the 2060s with a population of over 1.6 billion, as well as of the United States and Nigeria. Especially striking is the tremendous demographic dynamics in Nigeria; so high that it's hard to believe the accuracy of UN forecasts that envision a situation in 2100 where the Nigerian population is as large as 850 million and the Chinese one is 'only' that of 1,050 million. Hence, the difference between the sizes of both countries' population would drop from the current 1,190 million to 200 million (*sic!*).

It is appropriate to add here that it is Africa rather than Asia where the population is growing the fastest in the twenty-first century. Nigeria is the most vivid example as it's inhabited by more people than any other country in the continent. In 2018, the population of this largest economy in Africa (GDP of ca. 1.2 trillion at PPP) fluctuated at around 195 million and, with a very high growth rate – 2.43 percent a year (in China, it's only 0.41 percent) – it will already have exceeded 200 million in 2020.[1]

It is worth realizing at this point what world we are living in; not all millions are created equal. Those almost 200 million Nigerians

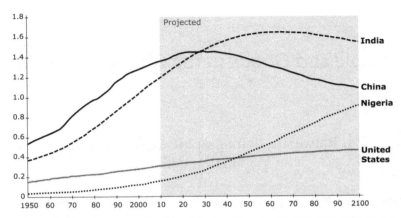

Diagram 9 Population of China, India, Nigeria and the United States between 1950 and 2100 (in billions)

Source: UN forecasts and data.

represent a very young society, a whole generation younger than the Chinese, as it is characterized by a median age of 18.4. In other words, in a group of 100 statistically average Nigerians, half of them are less than 18 years old; in a group of 100 Chinese, half of them are over 37 ...

Suma sumarum, the huge number of Chinese, now representing ca. 18.6 percent of humanity, should be viewed in the right perspective. While the population of the Middle Country is growing slowly and, over time, will start falling, elsewhere it is growing fast (too fast). Currently, Asia is inhabited by nearly three times more people than Africa, whereas in a 100 years' time, this difference will disappear completely, with populations of almost five billion people on each continent. Thus, the population of just one of these continents will be the same as the global population merely forty years ago, in 1987 ...

It is estimated that the Chinese will account for 14.3 percent of the world's population halfway into the century, and at its end, in 2100, only for 9.3 percent of the more than eleven billion strong human mass inhabiting the overpopulated Earth. A century is all it takes to move from a reality where nearly one in five of us was Chinese to a drastically different situation where this will be true of only one in ten. This should

Table 1 The world population between 2015 and 2100 (in millions)

Specifications	2015	2030	2050	2100
Africa	1186	1679	2478	4387
Asia	4393	4923	5267	4889
Australia and Oceania	39	47	57	71
Europe	738	734	707	646
Latin America and the Caribbean	634	721	784	721
North America	358	396	433	500
World	7349	8501	9725	11213

Source: UN forecasts and data.

be taken into account when discussing the far-reaching prospects of China's position in the fast and radically changing world.

Nearly all projections carry some risk of error. The same is true of demographic forecasts, though we are on slightly firmer ground in this respect. We know the birth and death rates, we know how many of us live and where, and we realize what average life expectancy the existing situation gives us. We are also aware of how many people migrate; not only from the countryside to the city but also from one country to another, beyond borders. But … there is no shortage of those 'buts', especially when we have quite a telling experience from the past. For example, that an Indian woman gives birth, on average, to almost two and a half fewer children than fifty years ago; the so-called total fertility rate (TFR) for the years 1967 and 2017 stands at 5.75 and 2.4, respectively.[2] Or that half a century ago a Mexican woman would give birth, on average, to as many children as an average mother in Niger, a record-breaking country in this regard, has today, because TFR used to stand as high as 6.81 and now it's only 2.24, slightly more than necessary to maintain the population level.

Let me add that maintaining a given society's population (again, leaving aside the migration balance) requires a TFR of ca. 2.2, 2.05 in highly developed countries, and more in less advanced ones. This is the so-called *fertility replacement rate*. We don't know how quickly, where exactly and to what extent these relations will change in Africa, especially in its sub-Saharan part. We can merely predict with a huge area of uncertainty.

Another big 'but' comes from the fact that each demographic forecast adopts specific assumptions as to the balance of migration; how many of us will leave the country of birth, how many of us will reach which country on which continent. This is also how UN population forecasts are prepared, also with respect to population trends in Asia and Africa. I have no doubt that the UN is wrong in its calculations, but I don't have any better ones that would be free of such errors.

The projections cited above, while making a couple of reasonable assumptions based on our knowledge of economics, society and geopolitics, are largely based on extrapolating a trend: things were and are that way, so they will be similar in the future. Well, no, they won't. Africa will not withstand the nearly 5 billion population burden in the early twenty-second century, and it's even doubtful if it can cope with the 2.5 billion burden in the mid-twenty-first century. If as many people are, indeed, born there as the UN predicts, they will not remain on the continent their entire lives but rather leave in advance. Few will go to Asia, so they will not be of much help to China in overcoming its population crisis. More will head for South America, even though it's far away, and the largest number will go – where else? – to Europe. It's close by, rich and there is already a shortage of people. One truly must be blind not to see the absurdity of the estimate that the ratio of the already overpopulated Africa to the underpopulated Europe will change from the present 5:3 (ca. 1,216 million and 743 million, respectively) to 7:2 in 2050 and to as much as 7:1 in 2100. It's nonsense.

Well, it will not change as in the meantime millions of people, tens of millions if not more, will leave Africa. They will go mostly to Europe, though it's recommended that we take actions to encourage many of them to migrate to the United States. It's one more reason to promote openness, tolerance and cultural pluralism where they are lacking and cherish them where they are weakened by the wave of growing new nationalism. Against this backdrop, the achievement of the German *Wilkommenskultur*, whereby Germany accepted over 1.2 million refugees and immigrants from Africa and Asia between 2016 and 2017, will, over time, look like child's play. Unless …

Unless Africa experiences a turning point similar to the one that was achieved in China, Mexico and many other countries. It's about tackling the previous trend of excessive number of births with family planning efforts. It's easy to say, difficult to do, but many countries of diverse cultures have proven this possible. It requires both a relevant national population policy and a radical change of mentality, which is heavily influenced by religion. The two predominant religions are, of course, Christianity, professed by ca. 45 percent of the continent's inhabitants (half of whom are Catholics), and Islam, whose adherents represent ca. 38 percent of the population. Without a radical change in their approach to birth control and family planning, the population issue in Africa may turn out to be impossible to resolve peacefully, which threatens disaster, not only in social terms and not only there.

We need to stop the demographic madness where over one and a half million new people appear on Earth each week, more than the population of Estonia or Bahrain, or of Iceland, Malta and Luxembourg combined. Today, at this writing, there are 226,030 new people; with 385,844 born, and 159,814 departed.[3] If the world does not come to its senses, this is unsustainable in the long run.

However, there is currently a different problem in China, as the family planning policy went overboard and now the aging process is speeding up. In 2010, young people aged 20–24 (with a growing number of students) were a 120 million-strong cohort, whereas in 2050 there will be only 53 million of them. In the same timeframe, the population of children up to age 15 will drop by 5.5 percent, whereas the number of elderly Chinese, aged over 65, will increase by 17.4 percent. Then, by the mid-twenty-first century, the median age in China will be eleven years more than now and higher than the current figure in the aging population of Japan (where, let me remind you, it's 47.3), rising to 48.7. Is such a country likely to conquer the world?

How can this balance itself out economically? How can this be sorted out socially? How can this be politically accommodated? Extending the retirement age, though absolutely necessary, will not in itself solve the problem. One may believe that a far-reaching robotization will be the antidote, but so far, even in such a technologically advanced country as Japan, it is not happening, or, to be more accurate, it is happening on a much smaller scale than was overoptimistically announced some time ago. Techno-fans are of the opinion this will substantially change.

It's a fact that the optimism of the 1990s in this matter soon proved to be excessive, and China played a major role here. Its entrance into the world economy as a sort of giant factory greatly lowered production costs thanks to the plentiful supply of cheap labor that was already available on the globalized market then. This resulted in a weakening in the push for robotization and automation as investing in them was not very profitable. Now – again thanks to China – the situation is reversing itself. There is no longer a mass of cheap but qualified labor and investment must be made in replacing it through technological progress. A quarter-century ago, millions of Chinese curbed the march of the robots; in the next quarter-century, millions of marching robots may help overcome the shortage of manpower. And that's why China, experiencing an increasing shortage of labor, is a world leader in efforts to robotize and digitalize manufacturing and services and to develop projects using artificial intelligence (AI). And again, just as in other cases, the fact that the Chinese are taking the lead in this matter makes some people glad, while others are worried, fearing Chinese expansion. Now, not only that of the human Chinese workforce but also that of AI-controlled China-made robots.

However, opening the economy, society and state to labor migration from other countries, especially those with a surplus labor supply due to the demographic dividend, will prove inevitable. Strong cultural barriers emerge here, posing a great threat of conflicts, as severely experienced by the United States, and even more so by Europe, failing to cope with refugees and economic migrants reaching their shores.

In other regions, this is also quite a problem, as some cultural barriers appear everywhere, but they are overcome in the face of the power of practical economic arguments, and traditional bonds. There is simply a need for workers, as in Russia, which hosts around twelve million immigrants, predominantly for work purposes, mainly from other post-Soviet republics, especially Ukraine. In the process, they send home a significant portion of their saved income, which represents substantial financial support, notably in Central Asian states. Countries such as Kyrgyzstan or Tajikistan would not be able to finance their current account deficit and their own budgets if it weren't for the economically significant remittances from Russia.

In China's case, neither is the Russian model applicable nor can the Chinese diaspora be counted on; even though it's quite sizeable, its economic situation in the host countries usually does not make it inclined to return to the homeland left behind generations earlier. Neither is it about the pseudo-opening of the economy for a workforce arriving from abroad, such as the solution used in rich Middle Eastern countries. In some Persian Gulf states, labor migrants even represent the majority of the population. In the extreme case, Qatar, as much as 90 percent of the workforce are employees brought from abroad, mainly from South Asia. Though nobody physically forces them to come, their working conditions and terms of employment are comparable to slavery. Even if that's an exaggeration, it's hard to suggest such a model as something worth following; though, to a certain degree (and let's hope with greater care shown toward the arriving employees), it will have to be applied in countries, which would otherwise fail to cope with the structural deficit of working-age people. China is already becoming such a country.

In the following decades, the Middle Country will undergo a deep demographic transformation, a much deeper one than its first stage, which has continued for over a decade now. From a country with a galloping population growth, which made the authorities adopt the drastic policy of limiting the number of children per family, China will become a state with a declining population. In most cases, especially in cities, until 2015, parents were only allowed to have one child. Now that this draconian discipline is gone, and the society has become wealthy, one all too often hears young parents, especially those from the new Chinese middle class, say that they cannot afford a second child. You hardly ever hear them talk about a third one. In a family – or in a household, as an economist would call it – a second car is sometimes more important than a second child. Of great importance here are also the growing professional aspirations of increasingly well-educated women, who prefer a professional career to having many or even two children. In the past, the state knew how to enforce the one-child policy, and now it is incapable of forcing parents to have at least two. This social and demographic syndrome is already casting a shadow over China's economic future.

To illustrate the demographic situation of a given society, we most often use the *dependency ratio*, whose value determines the ratio of dependants (people of non-working age) to working-age population. The first group consists of children and young people who are not yet of working age, and of retirement-age people. In the Polish statistical system, the 0–17 age bracket is treated as the 'pre-working' age, while over 60 for women and over 65 for men is defined as 'post-working' age. In other countries the working age ranges from 15 to 64, so people up to the age of 14 are treated as pre-working, and after 65 as post-working. The dependency ratio calculated this way is 37.7 in China and 52.2 in India. It could appear, then, that things are not that bad, but unfortunately the facts say otherwise; things are not good and will keep getting worse. This is because the Chinese dependency ratio is driven by a relatively low young-age dependency ratio, 24.3, and a relatively high old-age dependency ratio, 13.3. Meanwhile, for India, these ratios stand at 43.6 and 8.6 respectively.

If people could be circulated beyond state borders like commodities, the problem would be quite easy to solve. It would be enough to transfer surplus workers from the countries that have them to economies experiencing a shortage. For how many people of working age and in which South and South East Asian countries will the demand for their services be lower than their supply on the labor market, and consequently how many will be unable to find a job in their own country? Where is the situation the opposite, meaning they could potentially find a job abroad? These are dramatic questions.

The most acute shortage of working hands (and, increasingly, heads) is already experienced in South Korea, Singapore, Hong Kong, Macau and Taiwan, followed closely by China, Japan and Thailand. To keep the dependency ratio in these countries at the 2016 level in 2030 – and, mind you, even currently this ratio is inadequate – over 20 percent of the workforce will have to come from abroad. The problem is slightly less nagging in Mongolia and Vietnam, as well as in Brunei, Malaysia and Sri Lanka, where over a dozen percent of the workforce should come from abroad. Where from? Well, from the places from which the same amount of people should emigrate to keep the dependency ratio at the 2016 level in 2030. From this perspective, Laos and Nepal, followed immediately by Bangladesh, Pakistan and Bhutan, have working-age population surpluses of over 20 percent, and in the Philippines, India, Indonesia, Cambodia and Myanmar, the surpluses range from less than ten to over a dozen percent. These imbalances are a harbinger of a great Asian migration of peoples. Their intensity will increase, and the directions in which human masses will move will fluctuate.

However, people are not a commodity and they cannot be transported like banana boxes or containers of computers. Neither can we let things run their course and leave the matter in the hands of those concerned, as it would quickly launch an exodus from the first group of countries, the overpopulated and poorer ones, to the second, those with the increasing shortage of workers and greater wealth. What tensions we can expect in the future in this respect and what directions of mass human migration of tens of millions can be easily inferred from the information on the scale of the additional stream of working-age population required to at least maintain the current dependency ratio, and we know that it stands at an unsatisfactory level in many countries, including China.

Of course, these demographic forecasts – like all forecasts anyway – should be taken with due skepticism. Perhaps things will be a bit better than they seem right now. But they can also get a bit worse. It's good to know what will determine this, and where it depends on social and economic policy, as well as on education and upbringing, it's advisable

Map 1 Working-age population shortages and surpluses in South East Asia
Source: Own compilation based on UN and Taiwan National Development Council data.

to support the desirable directions of change and block those we fear. Technological progress may have a lot of surprises in store, either relieving, to some extent, the shortage of workers where it occurs or further aggravating their surplus where it's already a besetting problem. As a matter of fact, while Roomba, a computerized vacuum cleaner – sorry, iRobot – can alleviate, if only partly, the shortage of domestic staff in Japan, in Pakistan it can take someone's job away.

So there are, at the same time, too many and too few of us. It's no paradox, it's just yet another imbalance – a demographic one in this case – to tackle, though quite differently in overpopulated and underpopulated countries; in one way where the demographic dividend is high and in another where there is none. In a globalized economy this imbalance also takes on a supranational dimension and that's why the problem must be addressed supranationally. These are no longer the times when we could turn our back on the world ...

2. How long, how fast?

Problems with the low efficiency of some state-owned companies are mounting in China; a mismatch between supply structure and demand is becoming apparent, especially in the overheated real-estate market; many companies are in excessive debt and lose liquidity or have already become insolvent and qualify for bankruptcy. All this comes as no surprise, so there was sufficient time to properly prepare for handling these problems in terms of analytical work and theoretical considerations as well as from a practical perspective. Consequently, the economic policy attempts to address the mounting problems – for example, by means of further management decentralization, changes in the fiscal system and continued labor market deregulation (Huang 2017). In the West we keep hearing that it's too little, too late, that a loss of momentum is coming but it hasn't happened yet.

China is in for at least a couple of years, and most likely over a decade, of fast growth, over twice as high as the global average and three times as high as the average for wealthy countries; while for the world as a whole, this average stood at 3.3 percent between 2015 and 2017, for China it was 6.7 percent. Some believe that the boom will continue for even several decades more, but in my opinion this is a misconception. Except for potentially exceptional years, China will not go back to a two-digit growth rate, but despite this, it will be capable of quickly increasing its national income and, most importantly, the standard of living of the population. For how long? By how much?

It's a wider problem as other economies are also developing fast. For many years the 'Asian economic miracle' was discussed (World Bank 1993), with reference to both the impressive growth rate in the one-of-their-kind Singapore and Hong Kong, as well as in Taiwan and much larger countries such as Indonesia, South Korea, Thailand and Malaysia. Later on, Vietnam and India (the latter much more important due to its big population) also set out on a growth trajectory. Let me remind you that development processes will unfold in the foreseeable future in circumstances of peace. Let's assume that these countries commit no strategic error that would drastically bring their expansion down to a low level. In this case, how long can a fast growth of Asian economies continue, one that greatly exceeds the indices of other countries and regions?

The correct question, both in the Asian context and generally in economic growth theory and policy, is not for 'how long', as in 'how many years', can a fast economic growth continue but rather up to what level is it realistic? In other words, we should ask from which income the production growth dynamics relatively loses its momentum? If we know the answer to this question, we might venture to forecast how many more years respective countries can hope to dynamically continue to climb up the income ladder.

According to some authors (Eichengreen, Park and Shin 2011), a comparative analysis of past experience may suggest that an income threshold beyond which the march forward slows down oscillates around GDP per capita of 16,740 dollars at PPP. To be more precise, we need to add that this threshold is expressed in 2005 fixed prices. Fixed prices are a category we use for comparative analyses, though over time it is verified and then we use fixed prices set for later periods, having different structural characteristics. Here, let's assume for the sake of convenience that currently this threshold corresponds to a GDP of 20,000 dollars (PPP) in round figures. Countries with such income represent a sizeable part of the global community as there are 88 of them among 229 states and territories for which we have comparable statistical data.[4] Argentina and Iran, on one side, and Mexico and Lebanon, on the other, are on the edge, with the income fluctuating around 20,000 dollars (PPP).

Leaving aside poor economies, with a GDP per capita below 10,000 dollars (PPP), studies focused on countries where the average growth rate from 1957 onwards for seven years was no less than 3.5 percent and then rapidly fell. For this group, for seven years (as if the last fat ones), the average GDP growth rate was 5.6 percent before the threshold of 16,740 dollars was reached. Beyond that point, the rate went down to the average of the next seven years (leaner ones this time), that of 2.1 percent. This is a huge difference. At the rate of 5.6 percent, income is doubled in less than thirteen years, while at 2.1 percent it takes as many as thirty-three years to achieve it. Furthermore, for the former index it takes one generation to quadruple the income, while it takes as many as three for the latter one.

In South Korea, the limit of 16,740 dollars was reached in 1997. For the previous seven years, GDP per capita grew by 5.8 percent, on average, and in the seven years afterwards, only by 2.5 percent. In Australia, which was a whole generation ahead of Korea in this respect, for seven years before the 'watershed year' (1969) GDP rose, on average, by 3.9 percent and then by 1.6. In Japan, in the seven years leading up to 1968, GDP rose by 8.7 percent and afterwards by 5.0 percent. In Spain, until 1990, the figure was 3.8, then 1.6 percent. In Austria until 1974, it was 4.9 percent, and then over twice as slowly, by 2.2 percent.

There are exceptions that, well, exactly: do they confirm or question the rule? For the United States, fast growth continued well after the threshold of 17,000 dollars per capita was reached. This was due to the fact that the United States was and still is a strong economy when it comes to innovation and scientific and technological progress, which are powerful economic expansion factors. For the UK, once this threshold was reached, the upward economic trend luckily concurred with liberal structural reforms. In Japan, prosperity also lasted longer and the fast growth process continued until the early 1990s, mainly due to the successful combination of technological progress and export expansion. Hong Kong and Singapore, too, were able to stay longer on a fast growth trajectory, mostly thanks to being wide open to external economic contacts and trade liberalization.

Let me point out that all post-socialist countries that are EU member states have already exceeded the GDP per capita (measured, again, at PPP) of 20,000 dollars. In Bulgaria and Romania, the poorest among them, it stands at 22,000 and 24,000, respectively, and in the richest ones, Slovenia and the Czech Republic, at 34,000 and over 35,000, respectively. In Poland in 2018, this value is approaching 30,000 dollars.

Nevertheless, political commentators, politicians and some economists irrationally insist on parroting the opinion that there's a risk of falling into the middle-income trap. How can you get caught in such a trap if this level was already exceeded, in some cases quite a long time, over a decade, ago?

The information that, above such a threshold, GDP may allegedly rise by not much over 2 percent might be good news for the politicians unable to achieve more, but is that a fact really? Does it have to be so? Not at all. This is corroborated both by the experience of large countries such as the United States, Japan and the UK, and by various cases of small and medium-sized economies, which did not fall into that alleged trap. In each one of those countries, economic policy triggered new production growth factors, when the old ones were dying out, contributing to a greater propensity to save and to a high capital accumulation as well as to an improved allocative efficiency of investment. Specific favorable circumstances and good luck may help, but what really matters is strategy and policy, as well as progress in management quality at the microeconomic level.

China, now (between 2018 and 2020) reaching a middle-income level, is fully aware of this but will easily cope with exceeding it and will keep climbing higher. This is, among other things, due to the fact that already back in 2013, the Twelfth Five-Year Plan defined the growth path as well as economic policy instruments and institutional changes to balance the economy and avoid the 'middle-income trap'. It turns out that indicative multiyear planning can still be useful, provided it is well applied.

Why should the economic momentum stall at a national income of 17,000–20,000 dollars? What mechanisms are supposed to take away as many as two percentage points from the previous decent dynamics? It's quite a lot; for many countries, this would imply up to a 50 percent drop in the growth rate. Importantly, social psychology suggests that an annual income growth of up to 2 percent does not register in social consciousness. At least that is the case of countries that, considering their income, don't qualify as wealthy societies.

Two major mechanisms that cause the production growth rate to drop are changes in the economic structure along the urban–rural divide, and the fading beneficial effects of technology imports. At a lower development level, a significant impulse for work efficiency growth comes from a rapid flow of labor from agriculture (characterized by low labor efficiency) to industry, and these days also to the high-tech services. The fast economic growth once recorded in centrally planned socialist countries and in some 'Third World' countries came, to a great extent, from this rapid industrialization and the attendant urbanization. When a peasant becomes a foundry worker, growth rate rises. When a girl from the countryside becomes a seamstress, economic growth accelerates. Once a certain saturation level is reached, the process weakens and finally comes to a complete halt. In countries such as Poland or South Korea it has already happened, while in others, such as Peru or Pakistan, the process is still on. This is why, if not for any other reason, in the latter pair of economies (and in similar ones), we should expect higher growth than in the former countries.

Of course, this comment applies to situations where there are no special disruptions to the processes of macroeconomic reproduction. Indeed, as a result of the continued internal migration from agriculture to industry, one could expect growth to be faster, let's say, in Brazil or Nigeria than in Estonia or Malaysia. However, in the period between 2015 and 2017, total GDP in the first pair fell by 6.6 and grew by 1.9 percent, respectively, while in the second one, it grew by 8.0 and 15.8 percent. Things happen the way they do because a lot happens at the same time. The same mantra also refers to complicated business processes, and whether they yield a faster or slower production growth always depends on a juncture of circumstances. What greatly contributed to the economic recession in Brazil was a political crisis, and in Nigeria the low prices of oil, an export commodity it is excessively dependent on. Meanwhile, in Estonia and faraway Malaysia, the fast growth is the outcome of pro-growth free market economy institutions, prudent macroeconomic policy and skillfully stimulated technological progress. In the former cases, people move from the countryside to cities, but other factors impede the economic growth, while in the latter ones, such migrations are a thing of the past, but other causative factors have been set in motion.

Another mechanism involved in losing growth momentum at the higher levels of economic development is the weakening effect of the acquisition of technologies from abroad. As they say, why invent a wheel if somebody has already done it? It's enough to notice, learn, import, apply. Nowadays, it's no longer about a wheel but various branches of mechanical engineering and electronics, digitalization, nanotechnology, telecommunications, biotechnology and many other high-tech fields of production, and, importantly, services. The higher the level reached by economies, the lower the relative effect of technology absorption from abroad. In other words, if countries A and B have the same level of network advancement, they stand to gain nothing by importing from each other a technology they already have. However, if country C is lagging behind, then transfer of this technology may push its growth rate up, though this factor will only have an effect until standards converge. When country C reaches the level of A and B, its growth opportunities will be the same because the additional factor that previously accelerated its growth will be gone. How this mechanism works is clearly illustrated in countries that until recently have been developing fast and consequently have closed the technological gap. However, as a result they also closed one of the channels of accelerated growth. In Europe, we can already observe this happening in Slovenia and the Czech Republic, and to an increasing degree in Hungary and Poland, but for many more years it won't be true of Belarus or Serbia. In Asia, this can be seen in South Korea and Singapore, and to an increasing extent in China and Sri Lanka but not yet in the Philippines or Nepal, for many years to come.

In the process, a lot of misunderstandings emerge in relation to the determinants and consequences of the imitation- and innovation-based economic growth models. The proponents of the latter claim that the inability to transition from imitation to innovation is what condemns a country to fall into the middle-income trap. Far from it. Success in the form of multi-annual fast growth was recorded by more than one economy that knew how to make good local use of others' technological, organizational and marketing ideas that used to be treated elsewhere as innovation. Especially from a microeconomic perspective, on a company level, copying somebody else's proven solution, or the imitation strategy, is in many cases much more effective than experimenting with one's own innovations, or a strategy based on original solutions. This does not mean that a greater dose of innovation does not help dynamize the economy. It does, by all means, but it's not a necessary attribute. An economy can do without it, provided that it is able to drive its competitiveness by artfully imitating what others invented and implemented before. Also in this respect, China seems like an economy that is doing very well, or even brilliantly.

Today, a third mechanism is emerging that slows down economic growth in countries that are no longer poor. Namely, the more of them there are, and especially the more people there are in the world who enjoy ever-growing incomes, the more difficult it becomes to increase them due to the phenomenon of the decreasing extreme growth rate. It was easier to keep this rate at a relatively high level half a century ago, when the human population was just over three billion; it will be more difficult when soon it exceeds eight billion. Especially when more and more of them consume an increasing number of material goods, and the raw materials they are made of are not infinite, some of them becoming increasingly hard to source and more expensive. They cannot always be replaced with other semi-finished products obtained thanks to technological progress, and even if they can, the alternatives also cost a lot. If relatively few people were climbing the '20,000' hill, it would be possible to reach the top quite fast. If more and more people are working their way up the '40,000' mountain, their progress is a bit slower. When, one day, even more of them start to climb the '60,000' summit, they will find it extremely difficult. Any greater heights should be left to the few excellently prepared ones.

Per capita GDP in China is ca. 17,500 dollars at PPP in 2018, or is approaching the average global income. If China were to maintain the present economic growth rate, GDP would double and reach 35,000 in 2031. This is the level currently enjoyed by the richest country of the post-socialist transformation, the Czech Republic. However, it will make sense to point out that the Czech population is 10.7 million, while the Chinese one in 2031 will be 1,415 million... Can it be this way? Will it? What will happen next? Will China be capable of still marching forward at a fast pace once it reaches a development level close to the double global average of today?

Well, we shouldn't delude ourselves that upon exceeding a per capita income of around 20,000 dollars PPP, the Chinese economy will not slow down, but it will not be a 'hard landing', as the Chinese are able to land 'softly'. To make it happen, however, it's necessary to properly control the macroeconomic reproduction process. Chinese economists and politicians are aware of this and are making relevant efforts, mostly by dampening the investment boom to avoid overheating the economy and by moving the demand from outside to inside the country – that is, by replacing exports as the main lever of development with relatively faster growth in consumption.

Such policy of reorienting the growth strategy is slowly but steadily bringing results. That's why we shouldn't worry (or celebrate if somebody wishes China ill) that GDP in the second half of the 2010s is growing a bit more slowly than in the first one, because *per saldo* it's good news. Indeed, both dynamics and balance matter. It's not just quantity, but most of all quality that counts; especially if the society's basic consumer needs are already satisfied. Slightly slower growth should be appreciated, if it's a cost incurred to cause less damage to the natural environment.

Against this backdrop, taking account of the environmental limits to economic growth and the need to reduce economic dynamics due to the depleting non-renewable resources of the Earth, the prospect of the growth rate slowing down as societies get rich should be welcomed as essentially good news. If this happens, there will also be a chance to keep the environmental space for the high dynamics of emancipating economies and, mind you, most countries, not only China, still belong to that group.

3. Where is the East, where is the West?

I guess we could use a better compass. In addition to geography, there's also geopolitics, and in addition to both, there is also culture. No wonder that to this day it is not fully clear where the West ends and the East begins, and where Europe ends and Asia begins. When I asked about this on my visit to the Georgian region of Adjara, I was shown the border with Turkey and told: Asia is there. When I was traveling in Anatolia, in the east of Turkey, and asked where Europe begins, I was shown the same border and told: here it's Europe and on the other side it's already Asia. Yes, to some people Georgia is Europe, but not to all. Yes, to others Turkey is Asia, but not to all. It would be easiest to solve such dilemmas with a simple statement that all those lands lie in Eurasia.

I am fascinated by the division of the world that, due to historical circumstances, includes in the West the Middle Eastern areas that are the cradle of our civilization. So both Iraq and the Arabian Peninsula, and also part of Egypt, are in the West, and the East – typically of the east – lies to the east of the West (Morris 2010). This is a very original perspective, deeply anchored in history, because, after all, the West evolved from the Mediterranean culture, which would not have emerged if it wasn't for the earlier ancient civilization of the Fertile Crescent areas stretching from Memphis on the Nile River, in today's Egypt, to Ur in the south of Mesopotamia, in today's Iraq. However, sometimes frictions occur at the complex interface of the present day and the past, and people of today shift the locations of places at their discretion. It is the case also this time. After all, I myself was born in the East and now live in the West, though my country, Poland, has not moved one iota in the meantime.

And where is Japan? Not on a map but in reality. In the East, where apparently it has always been? Or maybe in the West, which it had already first partly joined a century and a half ago thanks to Meiji reforms and the attendant opening-up to external trade relations, then fully, coerced by the US postwar occupation, and next, out of its own accord? Or maybe in the East again, since the same is becoming a more attractive partner than the West? Certainly, it's in Asia and if we put it together with the continent's other emancipating economies, Asia's power is even greater. Just as Poland's occasional disagreements with neighboring Belarus don't change the fact that they are both European countries, so China and Japan squabbling over a couple of Diaoyu (or Senkaku, as the Japanese call them) islands in the East China Sea (more precisely over access to underwater natural resources, fishing waters and the nearby shipping routes) doesn't change the fact that these economies, which together generate more than a quarter of global production, are both Asian.

The West, the Euro-Atlantic one (without Japan and the Antipodes, including Australia and New Zealand), with its hubris and sense of alleged superiority, may, following the old maxim of 'two dogs fight for a bone and a third runs away with it', come to the conclusion that some internal Asian conflicts, as long as they don't escalate too much, could work to its advantage. Mind you, there are more dividing lines on the Asian continent than anywhere else. Scars remaining from colonial times, as well as unhealed wounds from the Second World War period and from several later regional conflicts, have an effect on bilateral and multilateral political relations, which is reflected in diplomatic relations and cultural exchange.

We can also see this in the tourism sector as these days it's easier to find Chinese coach groups in troubled Egypt than in South Korea, and there are more Japanese people traveling far from home in the Middle East than in neighboring China. The West, while extending its arms in business-oriented hospitality, should be happy that Chinese tourists head more in its direction rather than to the East. The westward tourist expansion does not have to be at the expense of limiting trips to the

East, to closer regions. There are plenty of beautiful and interesting places both here and there, so it's worth traveling to the four corners of the world. Moderation, once again, is best. However, Chinese outbound tourism to the West has been rising particularly fast, although from the Chinese point of view the Middle East is also West as it's both in the west and it's definitely capitalist.

In 2017, ca. 125 million Chinese people went abroad, the equivalent of the population of Mexico or France and Italy combined. When traveling, they spend a lot; in total, this already amounts to 25 percent of what all other travelers spend outside their countries. In just five years, from 2011 to 2016, the foreign spending of Chinese tourists increased more than three and a half times, from 73 billion dollars to 261 billion dollars. Credit Lyonnais Securities Asia (CLSA), a Hong Kong-based investment bank, estimates that in 2021 they will spend 429 billion dollars (Matthew 2017). If so, it can be assumed that as soon as 2022, their spending will exceed half a trillion dollars.

In the 1970s, many in the United States and Western Europe (the Eastern one was not back then visited en masse by such tourists) would grumble about the organized package tour groups from Japan, capturing, with their excellent cameras, historic monuments and the beauty of nature, and quickly moving on. The lovers of peace and quiet would say there's no greater calamity than an onslaught from such a group. Now, mass tourism is the domain of the Chinese and they are ten times more numerous than the Japanese ... Peace and quiet is nice, but shopping is good, too, as that's when business is performing better. When a Chinese person visits the United States, he or she spends as much as 6,000 dollars[5] on average, more than an American in Asia. Others, across the Atlantic, recognize this and also aggressively solicit more and more guests from the East. This time also in Eastern Europe.

What is of particular importance is that territorial claims and political feuds spill over into the economic sphere. And vice versa. They may seem to be only sporadic excesses, fuelled by the emotions of the hour (though often stimulated by governmental circles), but, as we know, things tend to get out of hand. In the summer of 2012, a series of demonstrations targeting Japanese companies in China caused a temporary shutdown of several plants that assemble Japanese cars, which involved a drastic decline in their sales. If this pleased Western European and North American companies whose sales went up, it was a short-lived joy. It is in the interest of the Euro-Atlantic system as well as that of the Pacific region, not only the northern one, to have peace and calm in the Asian system, including in the sphere of competition among processing industries, the successful negotiation of peaceful sea and land transport routes and borders, and armament issues. The West, while not directly stepping in, should use all possible means to favor a reasonable resolution of conflict situations in Asia as it is in the interest of them both.

This is by no means yet another clash of civilizations (Huntington 1996), as the problem goes far beyond just fierce market competition or even economic war. On the surface, we can see the United States vs. China trade and currency dispute or, more broadly speaking, one between the Euro-Atlantic West and the Asian East, but there are other underlying sources of discord. It's about much more than the fact that Huawei is a threat to Motorola, ZTE puts pressure on Apple, or Samsung has almost driven Nokia out of business. Or that India's competitiveness is increasingly making itself felt both in the processing industry and in services being the object of international transactions. It's not just about US fears that some sectors of their economy will be penetrated by capital from an Arab country, even a friendly one, as was the case with the intended investment in US ports by a Dubai-based company, a plan that was effectively blocked by protectionists from the United States, this alleged champion of the free market. The essence of the matter is the confrontation of free market capitalism – whose neoliberal deviation has totally compromised itself, causing the global financial and economic crisis and aggravating the conflict potential of the entire system – with state capitalism. It's about one more factor, this time a global dimension of the market vs. government discourse. This dichotomy is more important than arguments between countries and it will have an increasing impact on future development processes.

The US attack on Chinese companies is nothing other than one more attempt to make government subordinate to the market, or general public interests subordinate to those of private capital, while state capitalism strives for an opposite system where private capitalist interests are subordinate to those of the general public, though creating an alienated class of state bureaucracy in the process, which furthers its own goals. India lies somewhere in between and maybe it will be the one, rather than China, to chart the way for the rest of Asia. We are taking part in a show whose actors are wearing costumes: some from American vaudeville, others from a Peking opera and yet others from a Bollywood melodrama; the main characters' masks hide different faces. This clash will definitely have a greater impact on the future course of history than the outcome of the clash between Christian and Islamic culture, as some people think (Saunders 2012; Parekh 2013).

Just as there are several versions of liberal capitalism, there are also a few types of state capitalism. The European type, whose greatest stronghold is France, where government's involvement in the economy, measured with fiscal redistribution, is as high as 57 percent of GDP, could already seem like a thing of the past, though some believe that the new nationalism sweeping the continent in the second decade of the twenty-first century can still give it some impetus. However, it's a doubtful recipe for a better tomorrow. Conversely, the Asian type of state capitalism may be a thing of the future as it handles better than others the challenges posed by economic growth in the globalization era. The post-Soviet state capitalism, still not very well defined, and its milder Latin variety are looking for their place somewhere in between. State-owned companies account for over half of the value of the capital market in Russia and around one-third in Brazil; in both cases, such a high share results from the state ownership of large oil and gas companies. Which side of the Asian vs. Euro-Atlantic confrontation will be chosen by the emancipating economies of other regions will be of paramount importance for the future of the world, for shaping the global political and economic system.

According to dominant Western values, 'good' state capitalism is functioning in the Arabian Peninsula as it is pro-Western, while 'bad' state capitalism can be found in China, as well as in Russia, Iran, in Vietnam until recently, and in a couple of places outside Asia, especially in Bolivia, Ecuador and Venezuela (which is anti-West, especially anti-US). Adopting such a distinguishing criterion is yet another sign of double moral standards or, plainly speaking, hypocrisy. If we follow the principles of honest economics, what should determine whether state capitalism is good or bad is not somebody's biased ideological beliefs or particular economic interests but a pragmatic assessment, one made from the point of view of the impact a given system has on the triply (economically, socially and environmentally) sustainable growth of the country in question and on its effect on the external system – that is, on foreign economic entities. In this context, the Chinese model, and definitely not the Saudi one, seems attractive for many a country, and again (understandably) is treated by the West as a threat to its values, influence and vital interests.

Viewed from a broader perspective, state capitalism is gaining ideological and political strength because liberal capitalism is weakening, especially its neoliberal variety (Roubini and Mihm 2010; Galbraith 2014). The economic boom of many emancipating economies, on the one hand, and the economic crisis in the United States and in the EU, on the other, as well as the resulting shift of emphasis in the global policy coordination from G7 to G20, are changes of tectonic proportions. As with literal shifts in huge land masses, these are neither final nor stable. Even if, after such changes, the ground appears solid as a rock – and that's how it seemed to the empires of the Romans, Incas, Spaniards, Brits, the Soviet Union – there might come a moment when the land shifts again. And not necessarily due to an earthquake or, coming back to our context, a revolution. All it takes is an evolution if it's determined enough.

Let me remind you that G7 is a group of seven rich and large (with one exception) capitalist economies, which, until recently (the beginning of the twenty-first century), generated more than half of the world's production. That's why the United States, Japan, Germany, the UK, France, Italy and Canada (this is the exception, with a population of only thirty-six million), in the initial period of the contemporary stage of globalization, used to claim the world's economic leadership. Currently, it's impossible as they are no longer the seven largest economies; at PPP, China ranks first, India third and Russia seventh. Moreover, Indonesia and Brazil outrank the UK and France, Mexico is ahead of Italy, while Turkey, South Korea and Saudi Arabia beat Canada, which, together with Spain, rank only seventeenth and eighteenth.

The G20, this group of forty-three states, which is still in the process of spreading its wings and has no secretariat yet, is definitely more representative of the globalized economy than the G7. Exactly: forty-three, rather than twenty, as misleadingly suggested by the acronym, because G20 brings together nineteen states and the EU. Those nineteen are: Argentina, Australia, Brazil, Canada, China, India, Indonesia, Japan, Mexico, Russia, Saudi Arabia, the South African Republic, South Korea, Turkey and the United States, as well as the EU's largest economies – Germany, the UK, France and Italy. So, the G20 is made up of forty-three countries: nineteen founding members of this

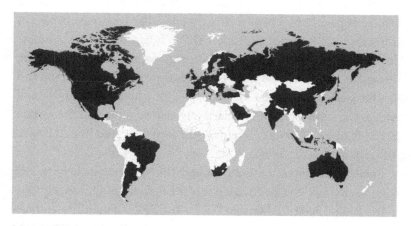

Map 2 G20 member states
Source: Own compilation.

loose association and twenty-four EU member states, to avoid double counting of the largest four.

The G20, bringing together ca. 63 percent of the world's population (the Chinese accounting for a quarter), makes up nearly 78 percent of the entire globe's production (the Chinese accounting for nearly a third) and generates ca. 90 percent of the world trade turnover.

As a side note, if G20 membership was determined only by the size of production measured with gross domestic product (PPP), then Argentina with its 2017 income of 910 billion dollars, and the South African Republic with an income of merely 760 billion dollars would be replaced by Spain with a GDP of one trillion more, 1.76 trillion dollars, and by Poland[6] with a GDP at PPP of 1.11 trillion dollars. However, in addition to economy, geopolitics matters, too, sometimes even more.

China, which hosted the 2016 G20 summit in Hangzhou,[7] is gradually strengthening its influence over the world economy, also using this forum for reinstitutionalizing globalization and coordinating supranational economic policy in a manner that suits it more. This will be the purpose of the new structures in which China takes part – for example, the meetings of BRICS, the group of five emancipating economies within the G20, where China is joined by Brazil, India, the South African Republic and Russia, and a special financial vehicle organized by China with sixty-one other countries, the Asian Infrastructure Investment Bank (AIIB). Interestingly, the Chinese distinguish between regional and non-regional member states. In the first group, they included forty countries from the Asia, Australia and Oceania region, and in the second, twenty-one states from Europe and Africa. Curiously enough, Russia, a Eurasian country, and the world's largest in terms of territory, is among the forty countries from the Asia, Australia and Oceania region.

Some observers of the Eurasian and US Pacific scene believe, not without grounds, that the AIIB is one of the elements of China's response to the Trans-Pacific Partnership (TPP). The TPP is a multilateral trade agreement, concluded in 2015 after long negotiations by twelve Asia and Pacific states: Australia, Brunei, Canada, Chile, Japan, Malaysia,

Mexico, New Zealand, Peru, Singapore, the United States and Vietnam. Quite apart from the fact that it is a valuable project promoting regional integration, which is surely a better response to the challenges of globalization than the new nationalism and resorting to the old protectionist practices, it is and has always been, geopolitically, an undertaking directly targeted against China. It has resulted in a major FDI decline in China, as some of the finance went to countries included in the partnership instead.

China, situated between Vietnam and Japan, on the western edges of the Pacific, would, in geographic terms, qualify for participation in the TPP, but it does not belong there geoeconomically. Or at least that's what Japan and the United States, the moving spirit of the agreement, decided. And, all of a sudden, what a gift! The new US president, hardly a free trade proponent, who, incidentally, opposes, not always for rational reasons, many phenomena, processes, institutions as well as cultures and states, pulled the United States out of the agreement before it was ratified by Congress. A strong aversion to free trade prevailed over aversion to China, though none the weaker. China cannot be displeased with this, enjoying again an increase in FDI from abroad. The TPP is being launched without the United States, but the AIIB has been launched, too. Also without the United States, because, even though the country was invited by the Chinese to participate, it was just out of political politeness rather than to see the offer accepted.

So China is missing from the TPP, but it can be found elsewhere. On this geopolitical and geoeconomic map of Eurasia, we cannot ignore the Shanghai Cooperation Organization (SCO), a still relatively loosely connected and very weakly integrated group of countries. The SCO was created at the beginning of the century by China and Russia with Kazakhstan, Kyrgyzstan, Tajikistan and Uzbekistan. Importantly, this forum for dialog and regional cooperation was joined in 2017 by India and Pakistan. In addition to full formal membership of the organization, a country can be granted the status of a dialog partner or an observer. The first group includes Afghanistan, Belarus, Iran and Mongolia, and the second, Armenia, Azerbaijan, Cambodia, Nepal, Sri Lanka and Turkey.

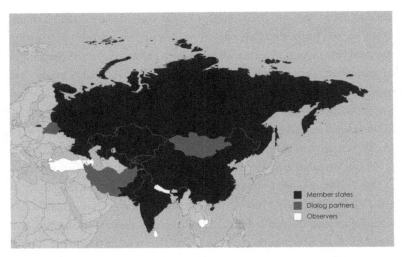

Map 3 Shanghai Cooperation Organization – member states, dialog partners and observers
Source: Own compilation.

The declared goal of this huge pact, the world's largest in terms of territory and population, is the concern for security in the Asian region, which is to be fostered by multilateral cooperation. It is obvious that China and Russia play a key role here. And again a question presents itself: should we count on the good fruits of this cooperation or be afraid of its consequences? We would prefer – at least the reasonable people of goodwill would prefer – those fruits to be as abundant as possible, but there are others who suspect this project of ill intentions and strongly fear its aftermath. So much so that they refer to the Chinese–Russian rapprochement as Donald Trump's worst nightmare (Andelman 2017).

Indeed, the political and military Washington DC may be afraid of the alliance between Beijing and Moscow, if it sees them as its adversaries, in the same way it used to fear such an alliance during the Cold War, the first one. At least until the Americans managed to seal the Sino-Soviet split, following over a decade of various ideological and political antagonisms, including a border conflict.[8] This was achieved thanks to effective US policy and diplomacy efforts, crowned by

President Nixon's spectacular visit to China in 1972. Now, something like this is impossible, especially as the Trump administration's anti-Chinese and anti-Russian rhetoric and policy is, despite his intentions, bringing China and Russia closer together. Of course, mutual visits are by all means possible, but a *détente* like then, is not, unfortunately.

4. Myth of the free market being perfect

What is 'emerging' or 'rising' is no longer markets, which are easy to manipulate, but a new world. Neither liberal nor state capitalism will win; neither the United States nor China; neither Asia nor the Euro-America; neither the East nor the West, as this is by no means a binary system. So none of them will be defeated. They will all have to learn to coexist.

China is becoming more and more appealing all over the world, while the West is losing its attraction in many regions. It turns out that more and more countries are orienting their monetary policy toward the renminbi rather than the dollar. When the dollar changes its exchange rate to the Swiss franc by 1 percent, Western Asian countries' currencies go the same direction by 0.38 percent. However, when the same happens to the renminbi, they follow in its footsteps by 0.53 percent. It is estimated that compared to the last pre-crisis years, in thirty-two out of fifty-two 'emerging markets' the reference position of the dollar declined, often to the renminbi's advantage.

In the context of such tendencies and especially in view of China's expected continued economic growth and growing share of the global trade, we can find forecasts predicting that the Chinese currency will become the world's dominant one as soon as in 2035 (Subramanian and Kessler 2012). I believe those expectations to be quite exaggerated considering that at the beginning of 2018 only the equivalent of 106 billion dollars of the world's currency reserves were denominated in renminbi. This represents only 1.1 percent of the total value of those reserves. Meanwhile, one should agree with the views about the inevitability of the importance of the Chinese currency in world financial transactions growing over time, both in relative and absolute terms.

China is becoming trendy, not only in the field of economics; it's also happening with respect to arts and politics. In the former field, a market bubble has even emerged. Three of the ten most expensive works of art sold in 2011 were painted by Chinese artists, including *Eagle Standing on Pine Tree* by Qi Baishi (1864–1957), which was sold for 65 million dollars. Admittedly, Qi painted beautifully but the anonymous investor has probably lost on this transaction by now; well, that's his business. In 2017, before it was revealed that *Salvator Mundi*, a painting created five centuries ago by Leonardo da Vinci, went for 450 million dollars to the Arabian Peninsula, to the Saudi crown prince, it was rumored to be hanging on a wall in a Chinese billionaire art collector's residence. These days, the stream of works of art going from the West to the East is bigger than that going in the opposite direction.

What should be the business of us all is the growing fashion for all things Chinese in economic policy. Another term, the 'Beijing Consensus', has become a buzzword in recent years (Halper 2010). For obvious reasons, it's being contrasted with the 'Washington Consensus', now being put out to pasture in economic history and pushed to the margins of mainstream political economy and economic policy. Still, is there any such thing as the 'Beijing Consensus'? Maybe it's another invention of Western economic and political sciences, as both these terms were coined in the United States, while the Chinese themselves are doing well without using this term? Yes, definitely so, though the term itself could catch on, as was the case of its infamous predecessor.

Incidentally, over a quarter of a century ago when the term 'Washington Consensus' was born (Williamson 1990), neither in the political nor technocratic circles in Washington was there any actual unanimity on how to deal with the outside world or, to be more precise, with the troublemaking 'emerging markets', first those from Latin America and right afterwards the Eastern European and post-Soviet ones. Then the concept of neoliberal market deregulation, an aggressive privatization of state property and the limited role of government became all the rage; it was dubbed an agreement and named after the city which was certainly one of the most influential places in the world, if not the single most influential one. The job was completed by the mass media and the fashion-conscious economists and political scientists who love to repeat catchy terms, even if they are imprecise and inadequate or sometimes simply stupid (Wheen 2004). Later on, attempts were made to modify this concept of economic theory and policy by adding an institutional layer and relevant social content under the new name of 'post-Washington Consensus' (Kolodko 1999b; Stiglitz 1998). Back then, two decades ago, it still didn't look as though Beijing could replace Washington and China would take over the role of the United States. Today, some believe this is exactly what's happening. It's wrong and surely premature to think that.

The case of the Beijing Consensus is similar this time to that of Washington because there has been no final agreement, in political or in technocratic circles in Beijing, on how to approach the outside world, especially other emancipating economies. However, since a certain line of China's outward expansion is becoming apparent and the Chinese system of values, different from the Western one, is pretty clear, we're getting a 'Beijing Consensus'. Its general interpretation boils down to the agreement as to the need for regulation of the economy, ensuring a significant state participation and the use of government interventionism, in which economic attributes go hand in hand with political centralism anchored in a single-party system. Again, the media and the economic parrot are doing the rest.

Efforts to westernize the world, and especially to Americanize it, have failed and so would efforts to Sinicize it, if any were undertaken, which is not happening. Just as some assessments of the Chinese economic reality are exaggerated, which sometimes reduce it to 'authoritarian capitalism' (McGregor 2012), so are the conjectures regarding China's alleged imperial ambitions. The illusory Beijing Consensus will not upstage the Washington Consensus, which is leaving the stage through fault of its own. Something else, better and forward-looking

(Pankaj 2012), is needed. This is all the more difficult because, since the intellectual, political and moral disgrace of neoliberal capitalism, no innovative and appealing idea has come forth that could fill the resulting void. New pragmatism is just a starter of a preliminary concept and there's a long way ahead.

Neither China, which is still searching (gladly drawing on the great Confucius, whose thought, however, cannot be the foundation of the future), nor anybody else in Asia or outside has a ready-made and satisfactory answer to the fundamental question of 'what next?' It's not about forecasts, not even the best ones (Randers 2012), but about outlining a more or less consistent vision of the future of the globalized economy, as well as theoretical and practical ways to pursue dynamically sustainable development along its lines (Kolodko 2014a; Rodrik 2015; Phelps 2013). What we need is a colossal effort not to throw away the baby with the bathwater and to protect the universal values of the West. Political neoliberalism is making a mockery of true democracy, and economic neoliberalism is turning the economy into its private farm, but this doesn't mean that we shouldn't cherish liberal values: freedom, genuine choice, fair competition, freedom of enterprise, market and social economy.

A multipolar world with multiple economic and political centers is being born, diversity of cultures is flourishing and none of them, not even one of the major economies, will totally dominate, with others receding into the background (Kolodko 2011a; Kupchan 2012). In this respect, there will be enough space for everyone in the future. Well, nearly for everyone. The world of the future will be a heterogeneous world and thus one that is culturally richer, and if we only manage to properly orient and control the permanent, never-ending dialog, there will be no destructive clash of civilizations but their creative harmony instead.

The face of the world in the twenty-first century and later will be mostly determined not so much by the outcome of the direct economic rivalry between Asia and Euro-America but rather by how these two megasystems of values, institutions and policies interpenetrate, and how they mutually enrich each other. The ongoing and intensifying confrontation is more of an opportunity for the future than a threat to it. We need to realize, however, that it's not only new markets that are emerging, as liberal capitalism would have it, but also emerging alternative ideologies are making themselves known. The faster this is acknowledged by intellectual leaders and the heads of all world political and economic centers, the better.

In a nutshell: the greatest threat to the rich Western world, as well as to some economies (called emerging markets by the West) that try to follow it blindly, doesn't come from China but from the myth of the free market being perfect. The wisdom of the East is not a threat to the future of the world; if anything, it's our one more chance for development in the future. The real threat is the lack of sufficient wisdom (not to say stupidity) of the West.

The world is moving toward multiculturalism and heterodoxy, and so economics should move that way, too. Neoliberalism's primitive *one size fits all* approach, adopting a single policy to all countries without taking account of their cultural specificity and historic legacy, and in isolation from geopolitics, is becoming a thing of the past. This is not the way.

The world of the future is a world of multiplicity. A multiplicity of cultures and traditions, but also that of preferences and visions; that of economic systems and types of economic policies. The world of the future is neither a world dominated by the Euro-Atlantic pact nor by China or, more broadly speaking, Asia. There will be no age of Asia, with the rest pushed into the background. The world will not turn flat in any direction (Friedman 2005), as it will always be round. China, with its huge dimension, will stick out above others but will not overwhelm them. There is no reason to be afraid and, on top of that, scare others with the 'Chinese dream', suggesting that it poses a threat to the global order (Mosher 2017). Americans once had their *American Dream*, so others have it, too. All people have the right to dream, don't they?

That's probably how the Chinese feel, subscribing to the *Zhōngguó mèng* slogan or the Chinese dream proposed by their leader (Xi 2014), and now they are trying to give it a practical content. Just as long as these dreams are realistic enough and not fulfilled at the expense of others. President Xi is urging people, especially the young ones, and he probably wishes there were more of those in the Middle Country, to 'dare to dream, work assiduously to fulfill the dreams and contribute to the revitalization of the nation' (Yi 2013), which should lead both to increasing welfare and to national glory. And to the flourishing of Chinese socialism. But that's quite another story ...

Socialism, Capitalism or Chinism?

1. Economy – society – state

The dispute over the essence of the Chinese system is not new, at least beyond the borders of China itself, as over there it's been consistently, as for three generations now, the country has declared that it's dealing with socialism. At most, this word would be accompanied by adjectives, which changed over the years, or synthetic descriptions would be added to characterize it. When I was in China for the first time, in 1989, I had no doubt that it was a socialist state, though, in many respects, that socialism was different from the one I knew better from the CEE countries. This was an authoritarian state socialism in a poor economy dominated by backwards agriculture. When I visit China these days, I do sometimes have doubts that it's still socialism, and, at the same time, I'm not sure that it is yet capitalism. When I went there thirty years ago, the middle class essentially did not exist, but since China started its great system transformations from the perspective of the economy rather than from, when I visit today, the energetic and entrepreneurial middle class, which is necessary for political stability and economic development, can be seen nearly everywhere.

So what are we dealing with? Is it simply a period of transition from one formation to another, or is it a different system, which deserves a name in its own right? After the system transformations that have already continued for more than a quarter-century in the CEE countries, there is a prevalent opinion (generally speaking, without getting into details) that the economic transformation has been a success, at least in the post-socialist economies that became part of the EU.[1] China, though, is following its own path. Where has it brought the country, where is it leading to?

The literature on capitalism and socialism is enormous. There is no need to discuss it here, though it's worth pointing out that throughout the entire time those systems functioned and confronted each other in practice, for most of the twentieth century, different meaning was attributed to those same terms, especially in intellectual, scientific, ideological and political debates. Such confusion regarding definitions and the lack of methodological discipline continue today. No wonder, then, that there has never even been a consensus in theoretical discussions as to what capitalism is, and especially as to what socialism is.

Those alive at the birth of capitalism did not analyze that period in terms of a 'transition period from feudalism to capitalism'; whereas this was precisely how researchers described the next formation, when they wrote about the 'transition period from capitalism to socialism'. Later, it would be added, ironically, 'and back', though building a post-socialist economy, society and state is not about going back to the *status quo ante*, but, instead, about a one-of-a-kind escape forward. As for a definition of capitalism, we would usually content ourselves with defining it as a socio-economic system based on private capital aspiring to maximize its profits (or, in other words, on the predominance of the private means of production) and free market exchange, whereas things were – and still are – more complicated with socialism.

The problem becomes muddled for many reasons, the major one being the confusion resulting from watching the same matter from different perspectives or different matters from the same perspective. So, for a political scientist, of key importance are the observations and interpretations of the ways power is gained and wielded, and of the functioning of the state and its institutions; whereas, for a sociologist, the heart of the matter is the society and the mechanisms governing the interactions of its component population groups. An economist, in turn, focuses mostly on observing and analyzing the recurring economic phenomena and processes and on explaining them, and if we go further – to normative (prescriptive) economics – on formulating recommendations for economic policy and development strategy. Meanwhile, all three use the same terms: capitalism and socialism, though they do not mean exactly the same. These words correspond, first and foremost, to an economic system, but they also involve obvious references to society and culture, as well as to state and law. As a matter of fact, it's not only the economy that can be capitalist or socialist, so can the society and the state. Furthermore, those distinguishing characteristics can be ascribed to mentality, too.

Of key importance is the fact that we once had real socialism, or the one functioning in practice – from the Soviet Union to China, from Poland to Yugoslavia, from Vietnam to Cuba, from Cambodia to Ethiopia. It differed, sometimes quite significantly, both in space – say, between Mongolia and Hungary or Albania and Czechoslovakia – and in time – say, between Poland of the first half of the 1950s and the second half of the 1980s or the Soviet Union in the times of Stalin and Gorbachev. But we had the same theoretical socialism, referred to by some – especially in the Soviet Union – as scientific socialism. This was socialism that was meant to be, that should have been there but somehow was always in short supply …

By the way, speaking of real socialism, it wouldn't be amiss to digress here and point out that it's the same with real capitalism. The one that exists in practice – entangled in crises, economic disasters and political manipulations, scandals over negligence and dishonesty, the insurmountable distance between the declared goals and the practical actions – differs so much from the one described in textbooks; or – if you will – the apology of this regime is at such great variance with the reality that we need an innovative theory of contemporary capitalism (Heilbroner and Milberg 1995; Ormerod 1997; Stiglitz 2007; Csaba 2009; Kolodko 2011a; Phelps 2013; Galbraith 2014; Tirole 2017), which would eliminate the chasm between what takes place in the real world and what is written about it in theoretical papers. This is one of the origins of what I call the new pragmatism (Kolodko 2014c; Bałtowski 2017; Galbraith 2018).

Socialist reality sometimes differed from its theoretic presentation so much that subsequent editions of the same academic works, being unable to ignore facts, were increasingly unlike the earlier editions. When comparing textbooks about the 'Political Economy of Socialism' by European authors published during one generation – in the 1950s and 1970s – the differences are substantial. Oddly and importantly enough, they differed between one another much more in Poland and Hungary than in Bulgaria and East Germany (GDR). The reason is, most of all, that due to various reforms that loosened the straitjacket of nationalized and centralized economy, the face of real socialism was significantly changing in the former two countries (also in Yugoslavia, which followed a different, but still socialist, path) and, coupled with those changes, its reflection in political narrative and scientific descriptions evolved as well. In countries that were less susceptible to reforms, the most orthodox ones being Maoist Albania (incidentally, the poorest country in Europe) and Romania, textbooks could be republished without major changes. It was similar in China and Vietnam, at least until the 1980s.

Allow me to digress here. I know of a case in the Soviet Union where, due to imperfect planning after the publication of a book entitled *Economics of a Transition Period*, there were stocks of unused covers left. Red, with gilded letters, because it discussed the period of transition from capitalism to socialism. Using those covers, in the early 1990s, a book with the same title was published, but this time it dealt with the period of transition from socialism to capitalism. I wonder if the stocks of covers have already been exhausted ...

Once, some could swear they lived in socialism; today, some think otherwise. Others used to believe they were on their way toward it; now they claim it was not so. One can say that over the years, the image of socialism in the literature on the subject becomes increasingly blurred rather than clearer. There are fewer and fewer cases where socialism can be found in reality, and, according to some authors, there are no more left. In this context, the case of China is, of course, the most important one. It is with respect to the Chinese case that the following opinion can be found:

> A plausibly socialist system would be judged on the following four criteria: capacity, intention, redistribution, and responsiveness. First, a socialist government controls a sufficient share of the economy's resources that it has the *capacity* to shape economic outcome. One traditional definition of socialism includes 'public ownership of the means of production,' but 'capacity' is here broadened to include the ability to control assets and income streams, through taxation and regulatory authority. Second, a socialist government has the *intention* of shaping the economy to get outcomes that are different from what a noninterventionist market would produce. Third,...a socialist government typically justifies itself as benefitting those citizens who are less well off...[through] growth, social security, and pro-poor *redistribution*. Fourth, a socialist government should have some mechanism through which the broader population can influence the government's economic and social policy, so that policy shows at least some partial *responsiveness* to the changing preferences of the population. (Naughton 2017: 3–4; italics in original)

Approaching the matter this way, the author concludes that 'China cannot be considered a socialist country until it makes much greater progress fulfilling its own declared policy objectives of universal social security, modest income redistribution, and amelioration of environmental problems' (Naughton 2017: 22).

Earlier on, Mario D. Nuti pointed to similar constitutive systemic characteristics of the socialist economy, also emphasizing the diversity and suggesting an interesting classification of types of capitalism and socialism.

He points out that the original socialist project was made up of four constitutive elements in different proportions:

a) dominant public property and enterprise,
b) equality and large public consumption,
c) economic democracy and participation,

d)   social control of the main economic variables (employment,
      income, accumulation, growth, inflation, internal balance, external
      balance).

He proposes considering only systems characterized by 0 = absence
or strong attenuation, and 1 = significant presence of each of these
four elements. Sixteen alternative models can be generated in this
way: some never existed, others no longer exist, others are still extant
(Nuti 2018b: 2–3).

In accordance with the taxonomy proposed, one of the variants
was socialism with Chinese characteristics, put in place in the 1980s
and 1990s; this is type 1101. Meanwhile, since the beginning of this
century, considering that state ownership is still dominant in banking,
which controls the access to and cost of investment credits, China is
type 1001, which is more associated with state capitalism than with
socialism. In such a methodological perspective, Soviet-style central
planning between 1928 and 1990 is type 1101, and Yugoslavia in the
period from 1950 to 1990 qualifies as 1011. Ideal social democracy, never
realized so far, is type 0111, while classical capitalism is type 0000. The
ideal communism – the utopia, which has never and nowhere existed:
without the state as the redundant coercive apparatus, with economy of
abundance, with universal shared ownership, with the rule of 'from each
according to his ability, and to each according to his need' – is type 1111.
One more reason why it's a good thing that communism conceptualized
in this way has only survived as a utopia is that it has saved the jobs of
countless economists, who, together with economic theory, would be
utterly redundant in an economy that is free of any contradictions. Well,
things took a different course and that's why we have our hands full.

Present-day Poland and Hungary – as well as the other post-socialist
EU member states – are already capitalist economies of type 0000,
while it can be seen clearly that this classification needs some nuancing,
which the binary system precludes. Indeed, someone else could insist
that those two countries – the erstwhile pioneers of market reforms –
are type 0101, considering the relatively low scale of income inequalities
and quite significant scope of social control over economic process,

which cannot be ignored. Of course, it makes little sense to add, let's say, 0.5 to 0 and 1 as then we would have as many as eighty-one variants rather than sixteen. Hence, when making a binary classification, it's better to complement the typology with a specific description to characterize the choice made.

So there are different countries – with their state, society, economy, culture and politics – that are referred to as socialist. Let's pass over, on the one hand, the fact that Nazi Germany was created by a party that, though fascist in nature, had the word 'socialist' in its name, embellished with the addition of 'national'. On the other hand, socialism is associated by some with something positive, namely with the social market economy of Scandinavian countries – Denmark, Finland, Norway and Sweden. In this context, to distinguish them from the CEE economies and from the Soviet Union, in Western literature (more often that of the political sciences than the economic one), the latter group is referred to as communist states and economies. This further complicates the deliberations as in this case we would have at the same time three socio-economic regimes: capitalism (for example, Italy), socialism (for example, Sweden) and communism (for example, Czechoslovakia).

This is not a convincing perspective, for a number of reasons (Walicki 1995). Well, communism also has many interpretations – from the specter haunting Europe, according to Marx and Engels, outlined 170 years ago in *The Communist Manifesto* (Marx and Engels 2014; Stedman 2016), to the so-called war communism in Russia almost a hundred years ago, to the utopian regime of abundance of goods and services and social justice, expected to supersede socialism one day. Throughout all the years of Cold War One, which was waged not only on the economic but also on the ideological and political front – and that's why it embroiled in its battles the social sciences, including economics and sociology – the reality east of the Elbe River was called 'communism' in the West, though in the East the term 'socialism' was predominant. So, those two different terms were used and abused to describe the same environment.

In most CEE countries, hardly anyone called the socio-economic reality of 1945–1989 'communism', as the same was only to dawn one day, whereas since 1990 the term 'communism' has been used quite universally with reference to the socialist era of those years, and 'post-communism' for the contemporary period, after 1989. This is unacceptable in scientific work, because there was no communism in CEE; there was real socialism. At most, we can assume that the Stalinist period until the political watershed of 1956 can be referred to as communism.

I myself had a few dilemmas about this, but they mostly stemmed from directing some of my scientific works to the Western public. Hence, the title of one of my books contained the word 'post-socialist' (Kolodko 2000a) and that of another 'post-communist' (Kolodko 2000b), though in both cases it's about the same period following the real socialist era. Interestingly, a decade earlier, another author, following his lecture at Harvard, used both of these words in the title of one of his books: *The Socialist System: The Political Economy of Communism* (Kornai 1992).

Even though science, with its rigor and methodological and substantive clarity, should be the discipline to define the categories we use and interpret, and explain the phenomena and problems we study, and then impose the correct terminology on mass discussions, frequently the opposite is true. While newspapers should more often use the language of academic circles, it is academia that borrows the language of newspapers. Certain terms, sometimes employed uncritically and without much thought, diffuse from the popular parlance into the scientific discourse and become widespread. This was the case with the terms 'post-socialist' or 'post-communist'.

The attendant confusion led to a situation where, in the 1990s, all of the republics of the former Soviet Union were treated as 'post-socialist', even those with a much lower share of private sector than the Polish economy in the 1980s, which accounted back then for no less than 20 percent of its GDP, and obviously nobody would refer to it as post-socialist. It's nonsense, when in 2018 we hear that Poland or

Hungary – countries with relatively free markets and liberalized economies three decades ago – were 'communist' in 1988, and Turkmenistan, having a lower share of private sector now than Poland and Hungary had back then, is a 'capitalist' country. Unless we go on to add that it is a post-Soviet state capitalism, a unique new category on the taxonomic chart of economic systems (type 1001, with post-Soviet characteristics).

In the meantime, nearly all post-socialist countries, including China – which itself still does not admit to being one – have been crammed into another category, mindlessly overused both by political commentators and in research papers: that of 'emerging' markets. So, here we are emerging – in Croatia and Vietnam, in Russia and China, in Kazakhstan and Serbia, in Armenia and Slovenia. So far, only Poland has emerged, since it 'will no longer be ranked by FTSE Russell as an Emerging Market (FTSE Emerging All Cap), but as a Developed Market (FTSE Developed All Cap Ex-US). This will place the country together with twenty-four other nations including Germany, France, Japan and Australia. Poland is the first CEE economy to be upgraded to Developed Market status' (Emerging Europe 2017).

The 'emerging market' is no longer socialism with its lack of free market mechanism, but it's not yet capitalism with its mature market, either. When approaching the issue this way, the socialism–capitalism antinomy loses its validity as what essentially matters is whether the market works or not. Instead, the discussion shifts from the plane laden with heavy ideological and political baggage (transition period between two systems) into the plane of more practically oriented disputes. Hence, less emotion and political intransigence than in the capitalism or socialism dispute can be found in the debate as to whether in present-day China, but also in countries such as Uzbekistan or Azerbaijan, we are dealing with a reformed planned economy or a market economy, on the one hand, or, on the other hand, is this still a state economy or already a private one.

That's why, further on, I pass over those taxonomically important dilemmas and, not to complicate things even more, I will only make a side observation that one of the US presidential candidates in 2016, Bernie Sanders, called himself a socialist, while Emmanuel Macron, elected president of France in 2017, used to be the minister of economy in the government of the socialist president, François Hollande. None of them, with their political views, would have been accepted into the parties that held power in CEE until 1989, or into the so-called Communist Party of China at present. I say 'so-called' because what kind of communist party is it if it openly accepts or even endorses the attributes typical of a capitalist economy: private capital's pursuit of profit, a high unemployment rate, major areas of social exclusion and huge income inequalities, much higher than in many capitalist countries.[2]

This by no means exhausts the confusion over the application of the terms 'socialism' and 'socialist', as there once was the idea of utopian socialism, spawned, among others, by the Frenchmen Henri de Saint-Simon (1760–1825) and Charles Fourier (1772–1837), and the attempts to implement it, for example by the same Fourier in the *La Réunion* colony in Texas or by Robert Owen (1771–1858) from Wales, first in New Lanark in Scotland, and then also in the United States. It is fitting to add that there is also no shortage of utopian socialists these days, though, due to the past disgrace of real socialism, and the current poor social resonance of the leftist program, they get almost no traction. This is shown by the results of the recent elections in several European countries, where parties with a socialist orientation – also Labor and Social Democratic – used to do quite well.

Last but not least, presently we have hybrid and poorly performing, or even crisis-prone, systems, which are called socialism by their detractors, authors and proponents alike. I'm not talking here about the caricature of socialism as practiced by former president of Zimbabwe, Robert Mugabe, who, at the beginning of this century, declared his willingness to introduce a centrally controlled economy, while in fact his policy allowed extremely corrupt state capitalism to boom; rather than that I mean the more noteworthy Latin American experiments, such as *socialismo del siglo XXI* of Hugo Chávez and his successor as the president of Venezuela, Nicolás Maduro, or *socialismo del siglo XXI* in Bolivia, Ecuador and Nicaragua. These are mixed systems, pervaded with elements of a policy associated by some with socialism, but in essence it is a socially oriented capitalist economy, which functions in less economically developed countries. José 'Pepe' Mujica, once a Tupamaros guerrilla, later (2010–2015) the leftist president of Uruguay, says that 'There's a fundamental problem there – you can't make socialism by decree. We on the left have the tendency of falling in love with whatever it is we dream about, and then we confuse it with reality' (Anderson 2017: 42). Maduro himself, seeing how wretched the results of the Venezuelan version of *socialismo del siglo XXI* are, concludes: 'Speaking about the working class, Marx said that time was needed to change history. Marx was right. It's a long struggle' (Anderson 2017: 53). It would take longer than the available time we have left …

The term 'mixed systems' has already been mentioned. It suggests that the problem is not about the choice between the stark alternatives: capitalism or socialism. While relevant discussion with respect to the poor (GDP per capita at PPP of 7,500 dollars) and small (population of eleven million) Bolivia is certainly engaging, with respect to China, rapidly getting richer and populous, it is fascinating. Bolivia will not affect the fate of mankind. There is no way China won't affect it (Kissinger 2011, 2014; Shambaugh 2016; Kolodko 2017).

2. In search of equilibrium

In textbook socialism, effective central planning ensured economic equilibrium; however, in the real world, as experienced by hundreds of millions of people, this equilibrium was always in shortage. The nationalization of property was meant to eradicate private property as a source and mechanism of exploitation, and to ensure harmonious development, while in reality it paved the way for an investment policy based on desires rather than on hard facts and for monopolist practices that threw the economic system off balance. Worse yet, instead of the equilibrium and harmony, emphasized in textbook economics (Lange 1963, 1971), what was observed in practice was quite regular endogenous growth fluctuations, which indicated their cyclical nature (Bauer 1978; Kolodko 1986b). It is needless to add that proving a de facto cyclical nature of the macroeconomic reproduction process in a socialist economy, hypothetically balanced thanks to central planning, contradicted the then official ideology and political economy of mainstream socialism.

Shortages occurred in all socialist countries – that is, in economies based on the predominance and sometimes even omnipotence of state ownership, central planning of the volume and structure of production, and wage and price control. There was a permanent surplus of the flow of demand over the flow of supply, with all of its negative consequences. This applied both to the sphere of production (enterprise sector), where shortages disrupted the continuity of production, contributing to lower efficiency than in the alternative scenario of equilibrium (Kornai 1971), and to the sphere of consumption (household sector), which took an especially heavy toll on the population. The scale of shortages was varied, and temporally and spatially diverse. It was less acute in countries that did not experiment with even partial price liberalization, and, at the same time, had rigorous wage and price control in place, in Czechoslovakia and the GDR, and the most severe as a result of inconsistent reforms in Poland in the late 1980s (Kolodko 2000a).

The word 'shortage' was foreign to economics textbooks in real socialism countries until János Kornai (1980) gave it a status as one of the fundamental categories of a centrally planned socialist economy. Furthermore, he pointed to the inextricable link between those two economic categories – socialism and shortage. If there's socialism, there are shortages. If there are shortages, there is socialism.[3]

Though in no economy of the CEE region, let alone in the Soviet Union, with its insistence on heavy industry and engaging in high armament expenditure, were shortages successfully eradicated, periodically there were times where the supply of consumer goods was relatively suitable and close to equilibrium. This was not a full-fledged consumer's market, which would ensure sovereignty of the same, but it was not yet a drastic economy of shortages. This was a producer's market as, with a relatively narrow supply offered, the producer dictated to the consumer what to buy. The state of full, ideal market equilibrium occurs – only theoretically – at market-clearing prices; all supply (Ψ) is sold, all demand (Π) is satisfied:

$$\Pi_1 = \Psi_1 \tag{1}$$

A producer's market is a situation of a slight surplus of the flow of demand over the flow of supply. It results in inconveniences, such as having to buy merchandise of a lower quality and forced substitution – for example, buying a couch with burgundy upholstery, not with the desired beige, or warm rather than cold beer – or wandering from one store to another in search of the wanted item, which will be found in the end. Or:

$$\Pi_2 > \Psi_2 \tag{2}$$

A consumer's market means the consumer has an advantage over the producer, supplier and seller. One can pick and choose, be fussy or even bargain before the purchase is concluded. This is a situation where we are not yet dealing with structurally excessive stocks and wastage of goods because they get sold in the end:

$$\Pi_3 < \Psi_3 \tag{3}$$

When the excess of demand over supply is high and structural, meaning a permanent inability to buy the desired goods, and when the extent to which buyers' time is wasted can no longer be tolerated, we are dealing with an economy of shortages:

$$\Pi_4 > \Psi_4 \tag{4}$$

And vice versa: when all the goods supplied to the market can no longer be sold – despite various marketing efforts and huge advertising expense – and part of them goes to waste, we are dealing with an economy of surpluses:

$$\Pi_5 < \Psi_5 \tag{5}$$

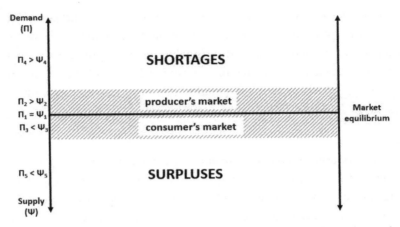

Diagram 10 Producer's market and shortages vs. consumer's market and surpluses

Source: Own compilation.

Crossing the fluid boundary between the producer's market and shortages was much easier than the returning process. It was also difficult to cross from the producer's market to relative balance. In Hungary, the latter was successfully achieved when, due to pro-market reforms after 1968, elements of a consumer's market emerged, and in Poland in the early 1970s – incidentally, thanks, to a great degree, to foreign consumer loans quite eagerly granted by the capitalist West. Therefore, the symptoms of the consumer's market were strengthened at the cost of generating an external imbalance resulting in a growing foreign debt, until it became impossible to service it in the coming years.

This was the situation in Poland in the first half of 1970s, but even back then we traveled from Warsaw to Budapest, thinking, not without a reason, that in this respect the situation was even better over there. However, when we couldn't find jeans in the right size and had to squeeze into a smaller size, or instead of the desired vinyl of Led Zeppelin we left the store in Lenin utca with a record of Procol Harum, even there we became aware of shortages. Of course, in market sectors that cannot be observed on the spot, with the naked eye – such as apartments, cars, phones, foreign currency for trips abroad – shortages were relatively much higher. Be that as it may, they were relatively low in Hungary, which makes it all the more interesting that the author of the theory of the economics of shortages is none other than a Hungarian economist, though Romanians and Bulgarians, Russians and Ukrainians, Slovaks and Czechs certainly had more opportunities to make relevant observations.

Unfortunately (or at least unfortunately for real socialism), the attempts to eliminate shortages by ensuring greater elasticity of prices and making them partly market-driven ended in failure. Partly market-driven because nowhere – not even in the most pro-market economies of Poland and Hungary – were they fully and completely deregulated.[4] This was not achieved even in China until the end of the 1980s, and the Chinese were smart to draw from it far-reaching conclusions. Without looking to socialist sister countries, they followed their own path. Without Eastern European shocks and without new leaps of their own, gradually, as Deng Xiaoping, the great Chinese reformer and leader, said, 'crossing the river by feeling the stones'.

By the very essence of real socialism, which dogmatically took care to ensure that prices should not be too high and intentionally guaranteed access to products and services to all population groups, pricing reforms could not have been effective. They partly consisted in the state raising prices to a level that balances demand with supply, and partly in deregulating prices and allowing them to be driven by a free market mechanism. When the unavoidable price increase was accompanied with moves to compensate the increased living costs, it was called 'price and income reforms'. This type of policy, which mainly dealt with the sphere of consumption as in the production sector the state's pricing rigor was much stricter, was able to temporarily improve the situation in the quasi-market. It reduced the symptoms of imbalance in the form of shortages, without eliminating the causes of this systemic disease (Kolodko 1986a; Nuti 1986).

It's appropriate to add that market shortages were not tantamount to depriving households of consumption opportunities, as stocks of goods moved, to a great extent, from, warehouses and shops to homes and fridges. To give you a better idea, on popular name days a local shop could run out of the desirable variety of vodka and dry sausage as a snack, but there was sometimes a surplus of those goods at the home of the person having the party... It must also be emphasized that a significant number of services for the general public were not provided on the free market. They were financed by the state budget and provided free of charge. In this part of the economy, shortages also occurred, but, naturally, they had no impact on the market.

Worse yet, in economies gradually moving away from the orthodox socialism model characterized by a high degree of decision-making centralization and strict bureaucratic price control[5] – a process that was already in place, with varying intensity, already from 1956, especially in Poland and Hungary, less so in Bulgaria and Czechoslovakia – the tentative reformatory measures in the form of partial pricing liberalization led to price increases rather than to the elimination of shortages. It was emphasized that:

> There is a causal relationship in one direction: the shortage strengthens the tendency towards (upward) price drift. But there is no casual relationship in the opposite direction... A constant price level, a fall in price, and a rise in price are equally compatible with the permanent maintenance of the normal intensity of shortage. Norms of shortage are not eternal, but no price change, in either direction can on its own alter them in the long run. (Kornai 1980: 498)

In addition to repressed inflation, typical of state price control,[6] open inflation emerged. The former resulted in households accumulating forced money savings, and the latter in price inflation, involving a classic increase of the general price level.

Meanwhile, in socialism that underwent reforms, both ailments occurred at the same time; something unknown to a free market economy, something quite unheard of in capitalism. For this dual inflation syndrome, partially open, partially repressed, I coined the term *shortageflation* (Kolodko 1986b), per analogy to stagflation: the coexistence of stagnation or slow production growth and the attendant growth of unemployment and inflation, which is known from capitalism (Haberler 1977). The scope of stagflation (SF) is conventionally measured as the sum total of unemployment (U) and price inflation (CPI) rates:

$$SF = U + CPI \tag{6}$$

whereas the severity of shortageflation (SHF) is expressed by the sum total of shortages (SH) and price inflation (CPI):

$$SHF = SH + CPI \tag{7}$$

Comparing the rates of stagflation and shortageflation, controversial as it is, makes great sense (Kolodko and McMahon 1987). In the former case, it's about choosing between the inflation rate and the unemployment rate, which dilemma is described by the Phillips curve (Fisher 1973), while in the latter, the choice is between the rate of price inflation and the rate of suppressed inflation, resulting in shortages, which is described by the shortageflation curve.

Without delving here into the methodologically complex issue of measuring the rate of shortages, it is reasonable to confront these two processes – as they are not so much situations as dynamic processes happening over time – because they show the systemic shortcomings

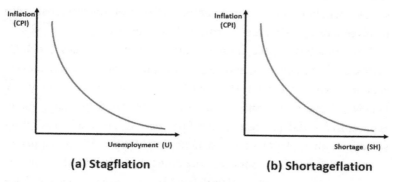

(a) Stagflation   **(b) Shortageflation**

Diagram 11 Stagflation and shortageflation
Source: Own compilation.

of capitalism and socialism. This real capitalism, in practice, cannot find the ideal that exists in theory, i.e. demand and supply equilibrium at full employment. In reality, it reaches at best the so-called natural rate of unemployment. This word 'natural' greatly irks some people because what is natural in this huge capitalist wastage that is unemployment?

> To this day, I cannot read without irritation (even outrage) that oft-repeated, canonized expression the *natural* rate of unemployment. Natural? Did the green Nature of forests and hares, rocks and earthquakes decree at the same time that there should be unemployment? I have been for decades a sharp critic of the socialist system, but friends and enemies alike of it should realize that it was marked by a chronic shortage of labor, not by chronic unemployment and a sizable surplus of labor. (Kornai 2014: 92–93)

The proponents of the term *natural rate of unemployment* certainly don't mean to associate unemployment with Mother Nature; they just state the unpleasant fact that, by the very essence of capitalism, unemployment is its inalienable feature, one that is always and everywhere inherent in it. In other words, such is its nature .... Moreover, it provides a kind of absolution. It absolves the state and the policy implemented by its authorities of the failure to take actions to reduce the size of the unemployment rate, since the same is natural.[7] Likewise, socialism, in line with the theory of the economy of shortages, naturally involves shortages. In other words, such is its nature ...

Protesting against the simultaneously occurring queues and high prices, or shortageflation, and suggesting a transition to a free market economy, which quickly turned out to be a capitalist economy, many people – I guess the majority in socialist countries, including many economists[8] – did not realize that they were in favor of substituting structural unemployment for structural shortages. What happened is that post-socialist countries, dreaming of a balanced economy, one free of inflation and unfamiliar with shortages – a bit like Alice in Wonderland before going through the looking-glass – moved from the right-hand side of Diagram 12, from the disagreeable alternative

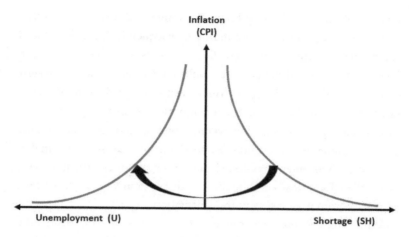

Diagram 12 On the other side of the looking-glass, or moving from the inflation-shortage alternative to the inflation-unemployment alternative
Source: Own compilation.

between open (price) inflation and suppressed inflation (shortages), to the left hand side, to the equally disagreeable alternative between price inflation and unemployment.

There is no way to stop at the intersection of the X and Y axes – without inflation, without shortages and without unemployment. So I think one should agree with those who say that capitalism is the lesser of two evils, being a system which, admittedly, does not guarantee dynamic equilibrium as it is characterized by permanent surpluses and underuse of manufacturing capacity, and, most of all, by unemployment, but, in turn, ensures a higher economic efficiency than shortage-plagued socialism, and, thus, a better long-term economic development and higher standard of living for the population.

When I look for a one-word answer to the question about the causes of the fall of real socialism, shortageflation is precisely that word. It's true that what greatly contributed to the collapse of the system was the autarchic development concept and the policy of isolation from global markets – first consciously embraced and imposed by the West – but it was the shortageflation syndrome that was eating away, like a cancer, this already not-too-healthy body of nationalized, overly centralized and bureaucratized socialist economy. Consequently, the lack of social acceptance for this regime escalated into its utter renouncement. The barbarous inflation, as some would refer to it, would so strongly erode the efficiency of the enterprise sector and reduce households' satisfaction with the volume of consumption, even though the latter was increasing in line with the overall economic growth, that not only did the societies of those countries stop believing that socialism makes any sense, their elites abandoned their attempts to reform it as well. The futile efforts to streamline the socialist system were replaced by a departure from it, or a system transformation.

When diagnosing the causes of shortages in socialism, the phenomenon of soft budget constraints is rightly identified as their source (Kornai 1980, 1986, 1990). Price manipulations – more often bureaucratic than liberal ones – were of little avail if they were not accompanied by the systemic 'hardening' of budgetary constraints, or adapting the financial streams flowing into enterprises and households to the economy's supply capacity. The supply of money was chasing the demand for money, and the latter was generated to the extent that could not be satisfied in the framework of state ownership of the means of production. If this property was a fundamental and, according to orthodox views, inalienable characteristic of the socialist economy, then shortages, too, became its intrinsic feature.

In our day and age, there is basically a consensus that in the case of Soviet and Eastern European real socialism, it was the state ownership of the means of production that caused the soft budgetary constraints, and these, in turn, caused inflation – more or less repressed or more or less open, depending on time and place (i.e. on the systemic and political context). That was the reality, but did it have to be inevitably so? While some claim it did, others believe that market-clearing equilibrium prices could have occurred in socialism without the need to introduce the regime of hard budget constraints (Nuti 2018a). And if this wasn't successful? Then it did not result from the essence of the system but from the deficiency of the economic policy. And of policy in general as the authorities did not want to fall into disfavor with workers, or with the masses, who, by default, don't take kindly to price increases, while the authorities of centralized socialist states saw this measure as a remedy to 'restore' the equilibrium, if they repeatedly failed to achieve this by increasing real supply. The word 'restore', commonly used in this context, suggesting that this equilibrium allegedly existed before, is put in inverted commas here because, by definition, there was no question of returning to the *status quo ante*, as the desired equilibrium was not there in the first place.

In the Soviet Union and in socialist economies of CEE, attempts were made but failed. Meanwhile, in China – as well as in Vietnam (Kornai and Qian 2009) and in the very poorly developed Cambodia and Laos – they worked. So, are market-clearing equilibrium prices also possible in socialism? Where it works, does it happen with hard or soft budget constraints in place? What follows from the evolution of the Chinese economic regime? Is it socialism with a balanced market, and, more accurately, with a market characterized by overproduction and unemployment,[9] as the stream of supply exceeds the stream of demand, or is it capitalism with still partly soft budget constraints?

3. Socialism with Chinese characteristics or corrupt crony capitalism?

The case of China is iconoclastic for at least two reasons. Firstly, if this is socialism,[10] then eliminating shortages in its framework has proved possible, without changing the regime. Secondly, if this is capitalism, then it can exist and, in economic terms, virtually boom without democracy.

These days, in China one can buy both a bowl of rice and the latest Ferrari model; it's enough to have money or the purchasing power, which is balanced in the market, on an ongoing basis, by the supply. Importantly, China was able to successfully get out of the economy of shortages without stepping into shortageflation, which devastated the economy of European socialist countries so much, even though, as yet, it has not managed to fully harden budget constraints. This is best evidenced by the mounting debt of the enterprise sector, fluctuating around 170 percent of GDP. Most of this debt comprises amounts payable by state-owned enterprises (SOE), or companies with a majority state shareholding. At times, banks, mostly state-owned ones, yield to the authorities' suggestions and are willing to grant soft loans to enterprises, whereas those enterprises sometimes have a hard time paying them on time, along with the accrued interest.

So, the case of China shows that it is possible to break free of the shortage syndrome by creating a liberalized price system and elastic price policy while maintaining a major SOE sector. SOEs function amid hardened, though still not fully hard, budget constraints. As with white and black, there is a whole palette of colors and shades between soft and hard budget constraints.

A free market economy is the necessary but not sufficient condition for democracy. Political correctness also calls for preaching the opposite view that democracy is an inalienable attribute of a free market economy and that, by its essence, it favors efficiency and, consequently, economic growth, though, in themselves, neither can the market eliminate dishonesty nor democracy preclude stupidity. Leaving PC aside, as it does not apply in science, which looks for truth, those propositions have to be at least called into question, if not dismissed outright. As a matter of fact, economic growth is promoted by right decisions taken both at the microeconomic scale, when managing enterprises where nobody is concerned with democracy, and on the macro scale, when running the economic policy, which, in contemporary Western-style capitalism, incessantly gets entangled in democratic disputes. It's not enough to be right (and those ruling as a result of democratic elections often are not), one also needs to have a majority.

At times of intensive and frequent economic and political changes, what matters is how quickly decisions are taken. The speed at which one adapts to the changing circumstances has a major impact on the effectiveness of management and economic policy. Enlightened authoritarianism has a positive impact on this speed, whereas democratic procedures need time for confrontations, discussions, negotiations and working out political compromises; all this is time-consuming, if not drawn-out on occasions. There are no direct relationships as decision-making mechanisms depend on many factors, including the procedures in use, the quality of institutions and the standards of the political class. Experience shows that democracy in itself by no means guarantees that and often it actually complicates the process of taking the right decisions. It's no accident that the financial crisis between the first and second decade of the twenty-first century was caused by the country where liberal democracy reigns supreme – the United States. It certainly doesn't follow from this that democracy should not be cherished; it should be, as it is a value in itself, even when it makes it more difficult to adopt rational economic solutions. It doesn't follow, either, that a lack of democracy favors economic growth. It can happen but it doesn't have to. And these days it happens rarely, China being a specific exception.

It is hard to quote other examples, apart from Singapore – until recently – and a few Middle Eastern states such as the United Arab Emirates, Qatar or Oman,[11] where the market is functioning pretty smoothly without democracy. It must be emphasized that this happens in the context of the clearly dominant role of the state sector. However, the fact that things have been this way to date does not necessarily mean that they will continue equally well in the future. The Arab Spring failed, but, after all, in some geopolitical zones there are even more than four seasons.

The otherwise laudable dismantling of non-democratic regimes did not contribute to maintaining a high growth rate, as revealed by empirical data for economies such as South Korea, Indonesia, Singapore, Taiwan, Malaysia and Hong Kong. The reason is that it was accompanied by a a lack of efficiency and ineffective decision-making processes with respect to macroeconomic policy and hence it could turn out to be less pro-growth than before.

Earlier on, the market functioned quite smoothly in fascist countries, in Hitler's Germany (Tooze 2007) and in Spain during Franco's regime (Townson 2007), as well as later, in the 1970s and 1980s, in Chile under Pinochet's dictatorship with fascist tendencies (Buc 2006). For a quarter of a century, South Korea – from the military coup of general Chung-hee Park in 1961 to the first free election in 1987 – is also a good (meaning bad) example of enlightened authoritarianism favoring economic expansion. This came, among other things, from a top-down dampening of the population's social expectations, which are free in a democratic state. In an authoritarian system, to say nothing of a totalitarian one, putting a damper on them can make it easier to modernize the economy, becoming, temporarily, a growth factor. That's why societies in such states may, for some time, be unaware of the losses – namely, the missing benefits of democratic freedoms – while appreciating the economic outcomes of a developing economy.

In China, even though its political system is not democratic, good things do happen. In terms of economic growth, the Middle Country is the greatest success story in the history of mankind. Something like that has never happened in the past on such a scale, and never will so much happen for so many in the future. The case of China confirms that of crucial importance to dynamic, long-term socio-economic development is the proper synergy between market and state, a creative harmony of market spontaneity and state regulation. And what 'proper synergy' means depends on the context. There is no single universal rule; every country has to work out their own synergy, taking account of the cultural, historical, geopolitical and environmental context (Kolodko 2014a).

China achieves this better than others. It's quite interesting that while some authors maintain this is due to socialism, others declare it happens in spite of capitalism; where some see the Chinese reality of the first decades of the twenty-first century as a social market economy (Berger, Cho and Herstein 2013), others grumble about crony capitalism (Minxin 2016). Where some insist it's normal socialism, others talk of the 'Chinese miracle' and state capitalism (Naughton and Tsai 2015). So what is it really: capitalism or socialism?

When determining the nature of a specific socio-economic system, many authors – at least since the time of Karl Marx and his *Capital* (Marx 1992) – consider property relations as the decisive criterion. Using them as a touchstone, they pronounce that capitalism has been in existence in China for over a dozen years, as, according to the data of the Organization for Economic Cooperation and Development (OECD), a greater part of the national income already came from the private sector at the end of the last century.

If such dynamics of structural ownership changes were to be maintained, at present the greater part of assets and, consequently,

Table 2 Proportions of private and state sectors in China (percentage of value-added, by form of ownership)

	1998	1999	2000	2001	2002	2003	Change
Non-farm business sector							
Private sector	43.0	45.3	47.7	51.8	54.6	57.1	+14.1
Public sector	57.0	54.7	52.3	48.2	45.4	42.9	-14.1
of which: state-controlled	40.5	40.1	39.6	37.1	35.2	34.1	-6.4
collectively controlled	16.5	14.7	12.7	11.2	10.1	8.8	-7.7
Business sector							
Private sector	53.5	54.9	56.3	59.4	61.5	63.3	+9.8
Public sector	46.5	45.1	43.7	40.6	38.5	36.7	-9.8
of which: state-controlled	33.1	33.0	33.1	31.2	29.9	29.2	-3.9
collectively controlled	13.4	12.1	10.6	9.4	8.6	7.5	-5.9
Economy-wide							
Private sector	50.4	51.5	52.8	55.5	57.4	59.2	+8.8
Public sector	49.6	48.5	47.2	44.5	42.6	40.8	-8.8
of which: state-controlled	36.9	37.1	37.3	35.7	34.6	33.7	-3.2
collectively controlled	12.7	11.3	10.0	8.8	8.0	7.1	-5.6

Source: Kornai 2008: 149 (after OECD 2005).

also production, employment and budget revenues would be overwhelmingly related to the private sector. However, this is not the case as the pace of private sector expansion was made to slow down in the last decade or so. In a way, it's natural as the fewer assets there are left to denationalize, the slower the growth rate in the private sector. That's one aspect; the other is that the Communist Party of China deliberately limited the scale of privatizing state assets, being of the opinion that keeping them in the state's possession, or at least under its control, will better serve the state's strategic goals, which, according to the party, boil down to developing and strengthening socialism rather than dismantling it.

One can estimate that the private sector currently produces not much more than it did over a decade ago and its share of GDP fluctuates around two-thirds. The official sources say that private business generates over 60 percent of Chinese GDP and provides more than 80 percent of the jobs. Fragmentary data from the National Bureau of Statistics reveals that in the first half of 2017, private sector investment grew by 7.2 percent compared to the first half of the previous year, representing 60.7 percent of total expenditure. At the same time, the considerable role of the state sector is emphasized. The value of SOE assets exceeds 150 trillion renminbi (23.1 trillion dollars), which is the equivalent of Chinese GDP for two years (according to the current market exchange rate), and SOE investment in research and development accounts for 25 percent of total R&D expenditure (China Daily 2017a). The China Public Private Partnerships Center, promoting the practical usefulness of public–private partnership, reports that in 2017 over 13,500 PPP projects worth 16.3 trillion renminbi (2.5 trillion dollars) were implemented.

There are no grounds to question these data, especially as we do not have any better. It must be emphasized, though, that because of the Chinese, the taxonomy of forms of business ownership has become even more complicated. The issue is very convoluted as in many cases it's hard to judge clearly: are we dealing with private or state ownership?

That's because even in this area there's a spectrum of in-between and mixed forms.

The solution to the dilemma of what is state- and what private-owned is often a matter of convention. The differences are not clear-cut, the distinguishing features of those categories are getting blurred, the boundaries are becoming fluid. In this context a special focus is placed not only on the traditional perspective on forms of ownership, but also on changes in the sphere of management and in state corporate governance. It is possible that actual corporate governance over somebody's formally private ownership is exercised by the state, and it cannot be ruled out that a SOE (more often one with mixed ownership) is managed by a private company, which mostly takes care of its own earnings rather than of the state's income and of furthering its other purposes such as employment, environmental protection or contribution to social cohesion.

It's symptomatic that when I was looking for current data necessary for relevant analysis, one Chinese economist told me: 'As the public and private sectors are gradually mixed together, China no longer emphasizes the ownership in most industries and stops publishing related statistical information. Therefore, it's not easy to calculate the share of those sectors in GDP. Many studies use, for estimates, information on the number of enterprises, fixed-asset investment, taxes, main business income, total assets of enterprises considered public or private.'

The multitude of forms of ownership in China – including the hybrid ones, which some authors qualify as private while others prefer to see them in the group of SOEs – is illustrated by the data demonstrating the size of employment and its changes between 1978 and 2016 in different types of enterprises. Nowadays, the Chinese government's statistical administration distinguishes ten types of ownership:

1) state-owned units,
2) collective-owned units,

3) cooperative units,

4) joint ownership units,

5) limited liability corporations,

6) shareholding corporations Ltd,

7) private enterprises,

8) units with funds from Hong Kong, Macau and Taiwan,

9) foreign-funded units,

10) self-employment.

Without thorough analyses and certain compromises on definition, in some cases it is impossible to explicitly decide if it is private property, or state-owned.

Meanwhile, what can certainly qualify as private sector is financial pyramids, of which there are more than just isolated cases. Despite decisive counter-measures taken by the authorities, efforts to eliminate them completely have not been successful; when one falls, another materializes. China is such a huge country that it would be surprising if it didn't also break records in terms of the scope of frauds based on the so-called Ponzi scheme.[12] The Shanxinhui financial swindle, operating for only two years (2016–2017), managed to attract as many as five million naive 'investors', and Ezubao caused losses of 59.8 trillion renminbi in 2015 (nearly 10 billion dollars at the then exchange rate).

It's worth adding that since the breakthrough reforms launched in 1978 by Deng Xiaoping, a major part of China's economic growth has resulted from the increased productivity of the non-agricultural sectors of the economy. However, such enormous economic success would not have been possible if it weren't for the fundamental changes in agriculture, where work efficiency also increased by leaps and bounds, though on a much lower scale than in industry. Both of these processes were accompanied by the greatest migration in history, during which hundreds of millions of peasants left agriculture and moved to the city. Currently, the urban population already represents the majority of the Chinese population, as it accounts for 58 percent.

Table 3 Employment in enterprises representing different forms of ownership in China between 1978 and 2016

(10 000 persons)

Year	Total	Urban Areas											Rural Areas		
		Subtotal	State-owned Units	Collective-owned Units	Cooperative Units	Joint Ownership Units	Limited Liability Corporations	Share Holding Corporations Ltd.	Private Enterprises	Units with Funds from Hong Kong, Macao and Taiwan	Foreign Funded Units	Self-employed Individuals	Subtotal	Private Enterprises	Self-employed Individuals
1978	40 152	9 514	7 451	2 048								15	30 638		
1980	42 361	10 525	8 019	2 425								81	31 836		
1985	49 873	12 808	8 990	3 324		38				4	6	450	37 065		
1990	64 749	17 041	10 346	3 549		96			57	272	62	614	47 708	113	1 491
1995	68 065	19 040	11 261	3 147		53			485	310	241	1 560	49 025	471	3 054
2000	72 085	23 151	8 102	1 499	165	42	687	317	1 268	326	332	2 136	48 934	1 139	2 934
2001	72 797	24 123	7 640	1 291	153	45	841	457	1 527	367	345	2 131	48 674	1 187	2 629
2002	73 280	25 159	7 163	1 122	161	45	1 083	483	1 999	409	391	2 269	48 121	1 411	2 474
2003	73 736	26 230	6 876	1 000	173	44	1 261	538	2 545	454	454	2 377	47 506	1 754	2 260
2004	74 264	27 293	6 710	897	192	44	1 436	592	2 994	470	563	2 521	46 971	2 024	2 066
2005	74 647	28 389	6 488	810	188	45	1 750	625	3 458	557	688	2 778	46 258	2 366	2 123
2006	74 978	29 630	6 430	764	178	45	1 920	699	3 954	611	796	3 012	45 348	2 632	2 147
2007	75 321	30 953	6 424	718	170	43	2 075	741	4 581	680	903	3 310	44 368	2 672	2 187
2008	75 564	32 103	6 447	662	164	43	2 194	788	5 124	679	943	3 609	43 461	2 780	2 167
2009	75 828	33 322	6 420	618	160	37	2 433	840	5 544	721	978	4 245	42 506	3 063	2 341
2010	76 105	34 687	6 516	597	166	36	2 613	956	6 071	770	1 053	4 467	41 418	3 347	2 540
2011	76 420	35 914	6 704	603	149	37	3 269	1 024	6 912	932	1 217	5 227	40 596	3 442	2 718
2012	76 704	37 102	6 839	589	149	39	3 787	1 183	7 557	969	1 246	5 643	39 602	3 739	2 986
2013	76 977	38 240	6 365	566	108	25	6 069	1 243	8 242	1 397	1 566	6 142	38 737	4 279	3 193
2014	77 253	39 310	6 312	537	103	22	6 315	1 121	9 857	1 393	1 562	7 009	37 943	4 533	3 575
2015	77 451	40 410	6 208	481	92	20	6 389	1 751	11 180	1 344	1 446	7 800	37 041	5 215	3 882
2016	77 603	41 428	6 170	453	86	18	6 381	1 824	12 083	1 305	1 361	8 627	36 175	5 914	4 235

Source: National Bureau of Statistics, Beijing.

This means that as many as 42 percent of the Chinese live in the countryside or, to be more accurate, in rural areas. Do they live there under socialism or capitalism? In both. A total of 314 million people work in agriculture; this is 40 percent of the country's workforce. However, agriculture generates only 8.2 percent of GDP, which shows how low labor efficiency still is in that sector. What mattered more to economic growth than the shift in population from agriculture to industry was the shift in ownership of the means of production from state-owned enterprises to private companies (Lardy 2014; Cheremukhin et al. 2015).

One of the causes for the relative backwardness of the rural areas is that, for ideological rather than economic reasons, arable land is still a collective property. It can be treated as a socialist type of property, such, land cannot be traded on the market, and neither can it become a source of income for the agricultural population. In Chinese agriculture there is no such thing as profits from selling arable land or the amassing of capital revenues due to the increasing prices of non-agricultural land, which would certainly cause arable land prices to go up, if it was commercialized.

Let us note here a fact often overlooked in the analyses, especially those emphasizing China's economic achievements, that not all paths are strewn with success. A major portion of society has scarcely, to date, benefited from the fruits of the overall giant economic leap. Places that are in full bloom neighbor those that are wilted; centers like Shanghai, which rivals, and in some respects beats, Hong Kong, or Chengdu, which looks no less impressive than Japan's Osaka, exist side by side with extensive small-town and rural areas that are underdeveloped or sometimes simply backward. This, on the one hand, results from decades of the dual policy favoring the fast development of selected urban areas, mainly in the south-east, situated closer to maritime routes, and of the export-oriented processing industry located there; and, on the other hand, it is the outcome of a greatly uneven distribution of the benefits of participation in globalization. Or, to put it more bluntly, this is the result of depriving large population groups of any advantages that can be reaped from it.

Interestingly, despite the enormous boom in the industry and services, the drop in the agricultural population recently slowed down. While in the years from 1997 to 2006 it declined by 100 million, in the next ten years (2007–2016), it only shrank by 28 million. In other words, in 1996 the agricultural population represented 36.3 percent of the country's inhabitants, whereas twenty years later, this index had decreased to 22.8 percent.

The view of China as a capitalist economy had already been formulated a decade ago, based on data on the rapid growth of the private sector, which gave it a majority position in the national economy. I myself maintained back then that, on joining the WTO, in 2001, China crossed a sort of shadow line when it comes to political systems, setting course for a full-fledged market economy (Kolodko 2011a: 229), and later I concluded that this is only possible for a capitalist economy (Kolodko 2014a). Some authors disagreed on principle, claiming that

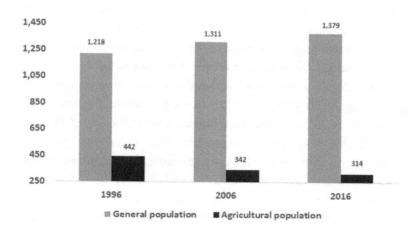

Diagram 13 Agricultural population in China between 1996 and 2016 (in millions)

Source: Own compilation based on data of National Bureau of Statistics in Beijing.

actually the case of China proves that it is possible to be at the same time a full-fledged market economy and a socialist one.

When speaking of a full-blooded market economy, I meant its more sophisticated and institutionally advanced form than the one achieved so far by China. It turns out that the path to a mature market is longer than we might think. The WTO still has not accorded to China the status of a market economy and, though a great majority of WTO member states are in favor of it, and rightly so, it remains unlikely, considering the obstructions created by the United States. Also, the EU is still reserved about granting formal market economy status to China.

While those with a more skeptical opinion on the Chinese economic, social and political reality point out practices in breach of the WTO market economy standard – such as exchange rate and currency market manipulations, restrictions on organizing free trade unions and strikes, huge corporate debt, overcapacity in some sectors, ill-becoming a decent market economy, and environmental devastation – others emphasize rescuing hundreds of millions of people from poverty and allowing, also by using market mechanisms, a wider range of society to benefit from the fruits of economic growth. While some are afraid that the great New Silk Road program is a manifestation of Chinese megalomania, others highlight the assistance offered by China to poor economies in their struggle to overcome backwardness, often one resulting from prior capitalist exploitation. While some get overenthusiastic about the advancement level and international competitiveness of Chinese private high-tech companies, others show cases of intellectual property violations or even theft, which are far from being isolated. While some argue that China is a functional meritocracy (Bell 2015) and China itself, speaking through the mouths of its governmental elites and their intellectual hinterland, talk of no less than the rule of law, urging the world to do the same, others focus on emphasizing that it's an authoritarian or even oppressive political system (Ringen 2016).

Such extremes are partly understandable, as concepts such as democracy, the rule of law or human rights are not necessarily taken to mean the same thing. In this matter, there are, at times, striking conceptual differences between China and the West that stand in the way of dialog, but the dialog should continue all the same. The views declared and, more importantly, the practices pursued are a contextual function of values, institutions and policies, and these, despite the Middle Country's far-reaching opening to the West, remain indisputably burdened with 'Chinese characteristics'.

For ten years now, the Economist Intelligence Unit has been compiling a synthetic 'Democracy Index', using a sophisticated combination of as many as sixty detailed indices relating to the political, social and economic situation as well as to culture and the media. Results for 167 countries are presented on a scale ranging from a theoretical 0 to an ideal utopia of 10. For years, Norway has been close to this threshold, with its democracy estimated at 9.87 in 2017, and on the bottom of the list are countries such as Congo (misleadingly referred to as a Democratic Republic), the Central African Republic and Chad, with Syria ranking last with an index of merely 1.43 in 2017. In China, according to this assessment, the situation in recent years oscillated between 2.97 in 2006 and 3.14 in 2016, to minimally drop to 3.00 in 2017.

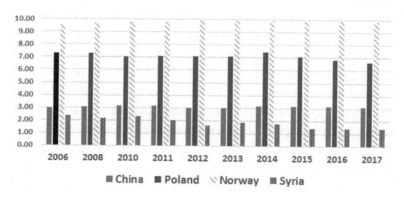

Diagram 14 Changes in democracy index between 2006 and 2017
Source: Own compilation based on Economist Intelligence Unit data.

For comparison's sake, we also show Poland, which features on this scale among the subgroup of inferior countries referred to as *flawed democracy*, with an index of 6.67 in 2017. Curiously enough – and, importantly, both in essence and from the perspective of the impact on international perception – this index fell in the period 2015–2017 by as much as 0.8 percentage points, from the unprecedented level of 7.47 achieved in 2014. In China, it currently stands at the same level as three years earlier and is not very different to that of Russia, whose democracy (or lack thereof) is estimated at more or less the same – namely, at 3.10 in 2017.

Hence, no wonder we have doubts as to how to define the contemporary Chinese system. Others don't, however, as they conclude that even though this is still a deficient market, it was already a capitalist system over a decade ago, deriving this declaration not only from relationships between core economic sectors – state and private ones – but also from the fact that shortages have been eliminated. Their judgment is clear: there are no shortages in China as it is already capitalism with hard budget constraints, which is demonstrated by the predominance of the private sector in the economy.

Opinions among Chinese economists on this matter are divided. An overwhelming majority of them publicly supports what the party officially declares. Off the record, they make no bones about being aware of more and more capitalist fundamentals in their surrounding reality. They approach the issue less ideologically and more pragmatically. Call it what you will, the heart of the matter is about efficiency and competitiveness rather than ideological and political disputes. They consider the WTO is wrong to claim that it is not a market economy as it's clearly a market with Chinese characteristics, whose essence – and, obviously, supremacy – the West is unable to fully fathom.

The issue needs a broader perspective, as the share of private ownership in the economy is by no means the only criterion for declaring socialism or capitalism. An equally important question relates to the nature and function of the state, and these can vary depending on the different levels of private production and employment. In specific cases, their share of

GDP may be relatively higher in country A than country B, but, at the same time, the nature of the state, its functions, tasks and activities, may determine that there are more elements typical of socialism. To settle the matter, one needs to take a broader look around. In particular, it's necessary to assess the scope of the state's involvement in the economy.

From this perspective, several types of states can be distinguished. Considering the tasks and functions of a state, four models are identified in addition to the classical socialist state (Block 1994):

1) public goods state,
2) macroeconomic stabilization state,
3) social rights state,
4) developmental state.

Without going this time into an in-depth analysis of these models, the names themselves lead to the conclusion that all these characteristics are present in China. The first two spheres – provision of public goods and concern for macroeconomic stabilization – are unquestionably a matter of state responsibility also in capitalism, something even neoliberal economists must concur with (though they will surely argue with their social-liberal colleagues over the scope of public goods). Meanwhile, the last two spheres – the area of social rights and developmental policy – are associated with the prerogatives of a socialist state. Or, which further complicates the matter, with state capitalism (Bremmer 2010). This shows how fluid the distinction between them is in some cases. Certainly, China falls into this category, unlike Middle Eastern-style state capitalism, such as exists in Saudi Arabia, or the Central Asian example of Kazakhstan.

On the long path from orthodox socialism to liberal capitalism, one that is longer than it seemed *ex ante*, there are many intermediate stops, the most significant ones being market socialism and state capitalism. To confuse the scene even more, they partly overlap; in this same place and time interval, something is there already and something else is there still, and yet something else is known to be coming, though it's not there yet.

4. Whither China and what business is it of others

China is actively getting involved in reforming the floundering global governance system. Since globalization is irreversible, the imperative for the coming years is to reinstitutionalize it. Undoubtedly, China will play a major role in this field (Xinzhen 2017), though this will definitely not be a 'globalization with Chinese characteristics'. The president of China announces that his country champions free trade and new-era globalization – not the one promoted by neoliberals, but one that is multilaterally beneficial.

Also this time, the Chinese imported a slogan from the West, talking of a *win-win* globalization. Cynics add that this *win-win*, which incidentally sounds nice and kind of familiar in Chinese, will mean 2:0 for China, but the idea is to have an inclusive globalization, in which China will undoubtedly play one of the leading roles in the coming decades. This is one of the purposes of the New Silk Road program, envisioned with much flair, and engaging both the state and private business. It is neither socialist, nor capitalist, but surely it's practical.

The growing global economic power of China is clearly visible from many angles. Not everybody realizes that the essential change in the structure of major corporations that has taken place over the past

Table 4 Number of state-owned enterprises from selected countries on the *Fortune* Global 500 between 2004 and 2016

Country/Year	2004	2006	2008	2010	2012	2014	2016
China	14	22	32	52	72	78	76
Brazil	2	2	2	2	2	2	2
France	6	4	4	3	3	3	3
Germany	6	4	5	3	2	2	1
India	4	5	5	5	5	5	4
Japan	2	2	2	2	2	2	2
Mexico	2	2	2	2	2	2	1
Russia	1	2	3	3	3	4	3
South Korea	1	1	1	1	2	2	1

Source: *Fortune* Global 500, 'CNN Money', http://fortune.com/global500, various years.

decade or so, toward more than doubling the number of state-owned enterprises among the top 500, was mainly due to the dynamism of Chinese companies.

While in 2004, out of 49 SOEs listed on the *Fortune* Global 500 (meaning they accounted for 10 percent of the list), 14 were Chinese companies, in 2016 in the group of 101 globally important state-owned enterprises (now they represent already 20 percent of that group), there were as many as 76 Chinese companies. And the question, again, is: is this a sign of the expansion of socialism or state capitalism?

However, the system evolution and the policy followed as part of it in the Middle Country will be subordinated to something other than creating the international power of China. What is and will be, in the foreseeable future, of greatest importance is an improvement of the internal economic situation. The Chinese expression *mei hao sheng huo*, which can be translated as 'better life' or 'happier life', was used fourteen times by the Chinese leader Xi Jinping in his opening report at the 19th National Congress of the Communist Party of China in October 2017. He emphasized that 'China's socialist democracy is the broadest, most genuine, and most effective democracy to safeguard the fundamental interests of the people ... We should not just mechanically copy the political systems of other countries' (Xi Jinping 2017). Dissociating himself from the *one size fits all* rule, typical of the neoliberal Washington Consensus, he added, with characteristic Chinese imagery: 'Only the wearer knows if the shoes fit or not' (China Daily 2017b).

Table 5 Changes in SOE presence on the list of the world's 500 largest companies between 2004 and 2016

	Specifications	2004		2016	
		Value	Share in %	Value	Share in %
1	Number of firms	49	9.8	101	20.2
2	Revenue (bln USD)	1342	8.0	5959	21.6
3	Employment (thousand)	8855	18.4	20117	30.1
4	Net profit (bln USD)	75.9	8.2	247.0	16.3

Source: Fortune Global 500, 'CNN Money', http://fortune.com/global500, various years.

Rightly saying 'no' to having shoes that are either too large or too small imposed on them, and being aware of its own memorable achievements and attendant strength, and at the same time sensing the needs of other countries looking for an effective path to development, China suggests that it may lead the way and that it will be a socialist one. 'Xi's vision of "a great modern socialist country", which aims for socialism's triumph over capitalism, not only guides China to avoiding the middle income trap but is a reference for the governance of other socialist countries' (China Daily 2017b: 7). At the congress of the party he leads, Xi Jinping said:

> The path, the theory, the system, and the culture of socialism with Chinese characteristics have kept developing, blazing a new trail for other developing countries and nations to achieve modernization. It offers a new option for other countries and nations who want to speed up their development while preserving independence; and it offers Chinese wisdom and a Chinese approach to solving the problems facing mankind. (China Daily 2017b: 8)

Depending on who rules where, political spheres' associations with the Chinese economic model may give rise to approval and recognition (though still rarely) or anathema and outrage (still more commonly). This is approached with greater calm and without excessive emotion in academic circles, especially in serious literature on comparative economics and development economics. If someone finds the influence of Milton Friedman's thoughts in Deng Xiaoping's policy (Harvey 2005), another can find in Poland's post-2015 economic policy the influence of the economic ideas of the Chinese economist Justin Yifu Lin. Such observation is not entirely nonsensical as in this case one can see the signs of the migration of economic thinking. Well, some elements of Lin's so-called new structural economics were inspired by the new pragmatism hailing from Poland, which is due to years of scientific contacts and cooperation.[13]

We are witnessing here an interesting circulation of economic thought on the harmonious coexistence of the state and private sector, market and economic policy, regulation and spontaneity, technology and culture, in highly diverse economic structures and levels of development. Justin Yifu Lin, who devotes a lot of attention to developmental economics, trying to put it on the right track, attributes a greater role to the state than I do in new pragmatism, but both these trends of economics highlight it, placing specific economic policy recommendations in relevant context (Kolodko 2011b; Lin 2012b). There is nothing wrong with being able to critically and creatively adapt the legacy of another nation's economic thought in one's own backyard: for example, learning in China from Poland's reflections and drawing on its experiences – and vice versa.

China is eager to borrow from abroad cutting-edge technologies, but also to use popular mental shortcuts or symbolic slogans. No wonder, then, that the chairman of the Communist Party of China rolled into one outlined a 'roadmap' for the coming decades. By condemning on principle one of the worst sides of the Chinese real economy, which is more associated by external observers with capitalism than with socialism – namely, the wide-ranging corruption for which as many as 1.4 million people (*sic!*) have been punished in various ways in the last five years – Xi Jinping indicated how, in two giant steps, China is to become in 2050 'a great modern socialist country' (Zhang 2017).

'Socialism with Chinese characteristics for a new era' already exists there, a 'great modern socialist country' is under construction. Party documents and official governmental materials don't reveal too many details about the creation of this glowing future, but we learn that soon, in 2020, there will be a 'moderately prosperous society in all respects' in China; then, after 2035, a 'socialist modernization' will be carried out, and in the following fifteen years, by 2050, a 'great modern socialist country that is prosperous, strong, democratic, culturally advanced, harmonious and beautiful' will be created (China Daily 2017b: 5). Everybody should be so lucky.

If we assume that we already have a social market economy in China or, as preferred by Chinese authorities, socialism with Chinese characteristics for a new era, then such an ambitious vision, of course with substantial reservations, may be worth considering. If we assume, however, that what we have instead is capitalism with Chinese characteristics, or even utterly corrupt crony capitalism, then we are faced with quite different questions.

I believe that deliberations such as capitalism vs. socialism with respect to China (mostly with respect to China but not only) are becoming less and less fertile and lead us astray. If every economist agrees with the view that the ownership of the means of production is of key importance to the way an economy functions, then every good economist must agree that of no lesser importance are culture, knowledge, institutions and policies. This, on the one hand, confuses the picture and the object of the analysis, and on the other hand makes the analysis easier as it enriches the field of observation by adding new elements. After all, things happen the way they do because a lot happens at the same time ...

One cannot but agree both with some Chinese economists (Lin 2004, 2012a; Huang 2017) and with critical external observers (Jacques 2009; Moody 2017), who show the *differentia specifica* of China and try to explain what and why is happening there without resorting to the system categories: socialism and capitalism. I myself am inclined to go in that direction, when formulating practical recommendations for new pragmatism also for China (Kolodko 2017). The key to understanding the heart of the matter does not lie in resolving this dichotomy clearly; it lies in challenging and replacing it with a sort of conjunction: socialism and capitalism rather than socialism or capitalism.

A toughening of ideological and political position is all the more interesting in a situation where new grounds for dialog are opening in the intellectual and academic community. We heard from the Chinese leader at the congress of the ruling party that 'Socialism with Chinese characteristics is socialism and no other -ism' (Berthold 2017: 31). Indeed, China goes with the momentum and several months later, in early 2018, it changes the constitution. Until now, the party's leading role was only highlighted in the preamble, now it's already emphasized in Article 1 of the constitution, which stipulates that 'The socialist system is the fundamental system of the People's Republic of China. The leadership of the Chinese Communist Party is the most essential feature of socialism with Chinese characteristics.'

Meanwhile, the Chinese president cum leader of the party having absolute power, Xi Jinping, when presenting his great vision of China at the National People's Congress's first session after the National Congress of the Communist Party of China, said that history had proven 'only socialism can save China' (BBC 2018f). This is one more controversial statement prompting historians, political scientists and economists to engage in never-ending debates on the past and inviting discussions of alternative history scenarios – what would have happened if… – and it must give rise to even more doubts about the future as it may prove neither socialist nor capitalist, or, looking from a different perspective, both socialist and capitalist.

I believe that the capitalism vs. socialism disputes are, on the one hand, a specific legacy of Cold War One, which real socialism evidently lost, as real capitalism clearly triumphed. However, this does not mean the end of history (Fukuyama 1989), as history will be with us for as long as we are surrounded by conflicts of interests and the attendant clashes. In Hegel's philosophy (Hegel 1956), ideas are of decisive importance in driving history, but in China's practice, interests are clearly beginning to take the upper hand. Then again, this does not mean an inevitable and constant confrontation between two systems whose fetters are so difficult to mentally break free from.

Some time ago, there were lively discussions over three alternative systemic megatrends and transformations:

- divergence,
- subvergence,
- convergence.

In the first, the opposing systems of capitalism and socialism supposedly coexist, and the challenge was to make this coexistence peaceful. In the second case, one system was to dominate the other and though many in the East believed for some time that socialism would be the dominant one, it proved otherwise. In the third case, a systemic convergence was to occur, with each system drawing on and assimilating some elements from the other, and thus they would become alike over a long historic process. Certainly, this partly happened as various systemic aspects of capitalism trickled into socialism and, *vice versa*, from real socialism into real capitalism, where they settled in well. This applies especially to the social reorientation of this system, which is, these days, so different from what Dickens described in *Oliver Twist*.

5. *Tertium datur*

China has, beyond any doubt, largely limited the scope of state ownership, though it is still predominant in the banking sector. At the same time, the division between public and private sectors seems blurred. Certainly, the kind of egalitarianism that the state attempted to impose in the Mao era no longer exists. Economic democracy and participation are restricted. The economy is subject to discipline both on the internal and international market, but, at the same time, the state maintains major control over economic processes thanks to traditional economic policy instruments (Tinbergen 1956), such as fiscal and monetary policy, interest rate and exchange rate management, price setting and SOE investment, as well as some forms of direct interference. That's why some authors believe it is justified to claim that China is an economy undergoing a system transition from subsequent forms of socialism to market capitalism. But how long can a 'transition' take? In post-socialist EEC countries, the post-socialist transition took a decade or two. What about China? Is it supposed to take a generation or two? Or maybe an entire century or two?

During the aforementioned landmark visit of US president Richard Nixon to Beijing in 1972, Zhou Enlai was asked by Henry Kissinger about the impact of the French Revolution on his country. Obviously, Kissinger meant the Great French Revolution of 1789. China's prime minister replied: 'It's too early to say.' This answer went down in history as an example of the unique Chinese ability to look at things from a very long-term perspective, that of historical processes. In fact, though, due to an imprecise translation, Zhou Enlai thought Kissinger was referring to the recent student demonstrations of 1968. It was only years later that the US Department of State's translator, Chas Freeman, revealed the misunderstanding, which he decided not to fix as it was 'too delicious to invite correction'. Even though this legendary answer can no longer be seen as evidence of Chinese long-term thinking, this quality is definitely something deeply rooted in Chinese mentality. Following this approach, it's still too early to judge what impact the collapse of the Soviet Union and the European post-socialist transition has had on the Chinese path to the future.

These days, China is undergoing a sort of convergence. It is experiencing a process of gradually infusing the social and economic reality with fundamentals associated with capitalism, but capitalism is being opposed or sometimes pushed out by elements associated with the mentality typical of socialism. One can say that an ephemeral form of socialist capitalism or – if you will – capitalist socialism is developing there; a sort of Chinism. Does this sound like *contradictio in terminis*? A contradiction in terms? By no means; we are just stuck in the mental trap of a clear but also false alternative: socialism or capitalism – *tertium non datur*. We need to free ourselves of this trap as something systemically different is being born; different but, in its nature, not entirely devoid of elements of both systems. Moreover, we can think back to the remote times when there was no capitalism or socialism, when the classical Chinese concepts of heavenly harmony, *yin* and *yang*, were born and the ethics of sustainability and harmony was pondered on, for example by the great Confucius (551–479 BCE). And then we can get back to contemporary times to see the elements of this approach in quite a different context in Chinism.

While not giving up on the specific values, differing in diverse places of this changing world, which always guide human beings and societies in their economic activities, and bearing in mind the imperative of caring for dynamic balance, what matters most from the economic point of view is effectiveness and pragmatism. That's what Deng Xiaoping meant, when he said: 'It doesn't matter if a cat is black or white, as long as it catches mice.'

Tertium datur.

Recipe for Crisis

1. At the expense of many for the benefit of few

At a time when it seemed to some that neoliberalism, having led to a widespread financial and economic crisis, followed by a social and political one, had been consigned to where it belongs – that is, to the trash bin of history – the same is rearing its ugly head again. It's no cause for celebration that in many places of the destabilized world, where neoliberalism used to be settled in nicely, it has been supplanted by a new nationalism and populism, more often right wing than left wing, oddly enough. You don't fight evil with evil, nonsense cannot be addressed with another nonsense. One has to make even greater efforts to offer something new, something progressive and socially attractive to replace those two harmful economic and political systems and the defective economic policy pursued as part of them. Undoubtedly, new pragmatism is one such proposal, but it will be a long time before it prevails (if it does at all).

What China is suggesting, a sort of Chinism, is definitely quite a different proposition than neoliberalism, though one can also encounter such original views as the one holding that Deng Xiaoping succumbed to its deceptive charm, when initiating his memorable reforms. Not at all true. One must agree that Deng liberalized the economy, but this had nothing to do with neoliberalism[1] as his intention was not to allow some to get rich on the efforts of others. Furthermore, he definitely did not intend to delegate major state prerogatives to capital and the free market. Quite the contrary: he aimed to use its mechanisms to increase the effectiveness of state control over the economy. It was his reforms that helped break free from autarchic development (Vogel 2013), something both the Soviet Union, and the Eastern European economies, more flexible in terms of system and policies, failed to achieve.

Worldwide, things run their course differently in different places, and at a time when China is consolidating its reforms, balancing its economy and trying to maintain high dynamics for as long as possible, the United States is apparently refusing to draw conclusions from its own mistakes. While China knows how to learn from others' mistakes, the United States evidently doesn't know how to learn from its own. This will backfire.

Currently, a decade after the outbreak of the devastating crisis (first in 2008–2009 in the United States and the UK, which has financial ties with the latter, then more or less worldwide), the professional community has no doubts that neoliberalism was its main underlying cause. It is an ideology, school of economics and, last but not least, an economic policy that, cynically feeding on such magnificent liberal ideas as freedom, free choice, democracy, private property, entrepreneurship and competition, favor the enrichment of narrow elites, with no regard for others. This goal is furthered by the kind of deregulation of the economy that puts the world of labor at a disadvantage to the world of capital, by the financialization of the economy, pushed *ad absurdum* at the turn of the twenty-first century, and by manipulating fiscal redistribution in a manner that favors the wealthier social strata. It was also furthered by the notorious tax reform in the United States under the presidency of Ronald Reagan, in 1986.

Suffice to point out that while in 1979, when Reagan was running for office (he was president from 1981 to 1989), the average hourly wage in the United States was 18.78 dollars (at fixed prices in 2008 dollars), in 2008, at the time the crisis broke out, it amounted to … less – 18.52 dollars! Whatever happened to the fruits of the major increase in labor efficiency, whatever happened to the national income growth? Well, as a result of neoliberal practices, they were captured by the wealthier income groups at the expense of those who are less well-to-do, even though their work substantially contributed to the overall national wealth increase. This is vividly demonstrated by other facts:

for instance, that between 1970 and 2010 the share of profits in GDP increased by nearly 10 percentage points, which is tantamount, from a different perspective, to a decreased share of salaries, which fell from over 53 percent to below 44 percent.

While in nearly three decades, from 1979 to pre-crisis 2007, the net income (after taxes and budget transfers) of one-hundredth of the richest Americans increased by ca. 280 percent, that of the poorest one-fifth of society rose only by ca. 20 percent. This equates to a truly meager increase of 0.6 percent annually, or in fact a growth much too low to be felt by the public at large. No wonder, then, that US income inequalities radically increased and now they are at the highest level among all rich capitalist countries.

It is precisely the growing income inequalities and the widening areas of social exclusion that caused people to first become angry and then take to the streets, also to the famous Wall Street, to occupy it. Things were aggravated by the irritating nonchalance of a section of the political elites as well as of the media and 'famous economists' furthering the agenda of those elites, who tried to put the blame for the glaring income and wealth inequalities – growing due to neoliberal practices, hence an intentional policy – on objective processes: on the current phase of technological revolution and globalization. This way, some of the anger was skillfully focused on aliens – on other countries and immigrants, on the Chinese and Mexicans, and elsewhere on Muslims or Eastern Europeans – and, as a result, on globalization, and another part on one's own establishment, which was by no means entirely blameless. And it turned out to be a power that brings waves of xenophobia, protectionism and anti-globalization resentments. It would be worthwhile to draw the right conclusions from this but, sadly, not everybody manages to do so. At least not in (still) the strongest economy of the world, the originator of the last global crisis, the United States.

As a matter of fact, a year after Donald Trump took power, a yet greater error is committed than the one 'achieved' by Reagan. A yet greater one because this time the moth still flies toward the flame despite the painful experience of the crisis of recent years, and when we should all be wiser with the benefit of hindsight. So should neoliberals, unless we assume that it's not about lack of wisdom, but about their boundless cynicism, which makes them advise and decide in full awareness of how bad the consequences of their decisions will be for the poorer majority. Unfortunately, neoliberalism's signature greed coupled with populism's naiveté – both characteristics uniquely combined by the current resident of the White House, which he blatantly demonstrates by running a neoliberal fiscal policy and populist trade policy – create a mix that is toxic for logical thinking and acting.

It turns out that, while you can never step in the same river twice, stepping into the same quagmire is by all means doable. That is exactly the path Americans are taking by pushing the 'historic', as they say, tax law through Congress. I call it 'pushing' because by voting at night, Republicans defeat the Democrats' opposition by one vote; because they succeed in doing so by buying off their own senators in return for evidently particularistic concessions;[2] because at the House of Representatives it's necessary to redo the vote as racing against the pre-Christmas time produced faulty bills.

While Republicans are pushing their propaganda of success, and President Trump is shouting 'Jobs, Jobs, Jobs!' from his Twitter account, writing that 'This is truly a case where the results will speak for themselves, starting very soon', Democrats unanimously protest against the tax changes passed, resorting to such drastic terms as 'assault' or 'scam' (New York Times 2017). Well, maybe not an assault as everything was done within the law and without breaking the Constitution, but it does seem like a scam in ethical terms.

People can sense what's cooking because only 27 percent of Americans support the new tax law and as many as 52 percent are against the solutions suggested and already being implemented. People can count themselves and they put more trust in the pragmatic arguments of non-partisan pundits than in biased pro-governmental experts and economists corrupted by the neoliberal lobby. While the latter are announcing a major economic growth acceleration due to decreased corporate income tax (CIT), independent centers – including governmental ones, some of which are really outstanding – calculate that the additional GDP growth by 2027 will be a negligible 0.4–0.9 percent, or next to nothing. According to the Congressional Research Service analysis, a CIT reduction by 10 percentage points (the law cuts it by 14 points, from 35 to 21 percent) can increase the long-term growth rate by a mere 0.15 percent annually.

2. Legally but immorally

So, what is the point of this battle? What do you mean, what is the point? To ensure that other changes jointly implemented under the trendy banner of tax cuts for companies help enrich the strata that are already rich. As a deputy prime minister and minister of finance, I myself used to cut taxes, including CIT, radically but sensibly: first down to 32 percent from 40 percent, the level applicable when I took office in 1994, after the infamous shock without therapy, and, upon taking office again in 2002, from 28 percent to the current 19 percent, after the needless overcooling of the economy. This, however, was accompanied by other changes, in addition to fiscal ones, that promoted not only capital formation and investment but also concern for desirable income relations and human capital development. Growth picked up pace, income inequalities dropped, long-term public debt did not increase. This will not be the case in the United States, though the reduction in the very high CIT rate, along with the simultaneous elimination of the many tax reliefs that impair the system, has its advantages. Growth will not accelerate, the unemployment rate will not fall, inequalities will grow and the debt will increase.

It is quite baffling how light-heartedly the authors and supporters of the US tax reform are treating the unavoidable budget deficit growth and the consequently increasing public debt, which is already immense. They are counting on China to finance it with its budget surplus, the way it has been happening to date. This is the case because a major part of Chinese reserves are held in US government securities. When the United States has a budget deficit or needs to incur a new debt to pay back part of an old one coming to maturity, the government issues bonds, which are an attractive debt security for others, those who have surpluses, and the Chinese have them all the time. It's attractive because, though it bears a very low interest rate these days, still it is commonly recognized as a safe investment. However, this is a shortsighted policy and a naive belief because a state of profound imbalance cannot be perpetually maintained.

With the exception of the apologists of the Republican fiscal package, there is basically a consensus that in the coming ten years the US public debt will increase by as much as 1.5 trillion dollars. And this debt already exceeds 20 trillion dollars, 7 percent over the US GDP.[3] It is not some anti-US extremist but a professional commentator who writes sarcastically that under Republicans, though they loudly declare themselves to be proponents of 'small government', this already giant debt 'is set to expand like the waistline of a middle-aged man who, after contemplating whether to exercise and go on a diet, opts to stay on the couch and eat' (Zurcher 2018). It is clear that in such a situation the Federal Reserve (i.e. the US central bank) may increase interest rates more aggressively, which will naturally weaken the propensity to invest, and slow down growth.

Democrats hope that the taxpayers seen as electorate by the ruling class and misled by government propaganda will quickly sniff out these neoliberal manipulations and already in the fall of 2018 their vote will strip the Republicans of the majority in both houses of the US parliament – the Senate and the House of Representatives. Maybe so, though not necessarily, as the way the tax package is structured, in the coming years lower taxes and reliefs will benefit a great majority of taxpayers, including those from less wealthy and more populous strata. However, their reductions disappear in 2025 and then the moment will come to pay for the cuts for the rich, which are not time-limited. Let's add that this will already have happened after the next elections, presidential, parliamentary and local alike. In total, throughout the entire decade of 2018–2027, the subsequent higher taxes, those regulated in the years 2026–2027, will neutralize the benefits of the earlier period, from 2018–2025. After 2025, as many as 53 percent of taxpayers will pay more to the IRS, and these will be households from the lower tax bracket.

Impartial analysts have calculated that the greatest beneficiaries of the reform will be the wealthiest, rich multinationals and commercial property owners. Indeed, one must have quite a nerve and display a reprehensible short-term bias in their economic and political thinking to push, in the context of what has happened over the last four decades, for tax solutions that will by no means cut taxes for the poorest 20 percent of the population. As a matter of fact, it is estimated that by 2027 their related benefits will total a mere 10 dollars, while for one per mille of the wealthiest, this will amount to 278,000 dollars (*sic!*).

Hence, it turns out neoliberalism, apparently still undefeated despite the recent crisis, is condemning the US economy to another, yet greater crisis, which is bound to break out one day. Its time will come when the scale of public finance imbalance disrupts the processes occurring in the real economy: production, investment and consumption. Worse yet, considering economic and social relations in their entirety and the cultural and political context, a major social revolt in the United States cannot be ruled out. As a matter of fact, democratic elections held from time to time, and freedom, including the freedom to publish stress-relieving hate speech in social media, may not be enough to discharge tensions.

This will not just affect the United States as, though the country's relative importance in the world economy will gradually decrease, it will still play, for several decades to come, a key part in world finance, and the US dollar will remain, in the foreseeable future, the main reserve currency. And that's why also others will pay for this new episode of neoliberal excesses. It is worth remembering who we will have to thank for that.

If the US economy takes another great plunge, it will be impossible to roll over its giant public debt without China's participation. One needs to be aware beforehand of all the consequences of this state of affairs as China has come up with a better idea of what to do with its financial reserves. Rather than financing the US deficit – i.e. sustaining US living standards, blown out of all proportion and impossible to finance within hard budget constraints – it will invest in pro-growth infrastructure investment projects in scores of other countries on four continents. Development economists, and especially the population of those countries, should not be worried by that, rather the other way round: it's something to be glad about. But whatever happened to the US strategists? *America First!* Seriously? ...

What Do the Chinese Ask About?

1. Right questions at the right time

At times, the questions asked of us are more interesting than the answers we give. And questions asked by others are certainly inspiring as they tell us much about what is of interest to others and why. Therefore, I always listen intently to the questions asked, problems formulated, issues raised. It's the same with China, both when it comes to talks held abroad and inside the Middle Country itself.

While traveling to and in China for the last thirty years, I noticed that professionals over there – those from academic circles and research centers, as well as within the administration and political community – have the unique ability to ask the right questions at the right time. Somehow never too early or too late. In the early 1990s, they inquired why our reforms in the 1980s had failed – well, they failed because it proved impossible to break away from the shortageflation syndrome – and the Chinese were able to draw practical conclusions from the answers obtained from various sources.

Ten years later, at the beginning of the century, they were watching different methods of state property privatization and its consequences, and, after all, hardly anyone contributed so much to this procedure as the Poles, with their numerous experiments. How shrewd! We were the ones to incur considerable costs of using various techniques, innovative at times, though not always effective, and they do not have to conduct such experiments as there had already been a lab elsewhere.

Another decade later, the Chinese were looking for ways to gradually liberalize interest rates and transition to their free market form. Lately, they have been looking into exchange rate liberalization, state administration decentralization or specific organizational forms of public–private partnership, among other issues. They are also following more and more closely what is going on in our neck of the woods, in CEE, with Poland at its center, as China is becoming more and more economically active here.

China has an outstanding network of research centers. They are located at numerous universities, but a large number of first-class stand-alone centers for research and analysis have been created as well. The Chinese like to refer to them as *think tanks*, as if convinced that it's yet another old Chinese term. Understandably, most of them are clustered in the capital city of Beijing, but many were established in several other large cities – from Shanghai to Chengdu, from Wuhan to Haikou, from Hangzhou to Tianjin. I get the impression that their work is cleverly planned and coordinated, hence the authorities, both central and local, have a steady inflow of valuable analyses and proposals for action at their disposal.

2. What students want to know

While the authorities ask about what they need for decision-making, students ask about what is of greatest interest to them. During one of the lecture series at Peking University, I meticulously wrote down all the questions addressed to me. I grouped them into some thematic bundles to show the spectrum of interests. Thus, Chinese students ask about:

Globalization and economic strategies

How should globalization be defined? As a continuous process taking place since the Roman times or as a contemporary process?

Is everybody doomed to globalization or is it a process that depends on a given country's economic policy?

In the context of globalization, is Marxist thought becoming stronger or weaker?

During your stay in Beijing, you took part in another Global Think Tank Summit. What topics considered there did you find most interesting?

Development strategy and new pragmatism

What is the role of ordinary people in making the world a better place?

To what extent does technological progress contribute to solving problems related to inequality, ecology and security?

How much does new pragmatism differ from China's current economic strategy guided by the concept of the 'black and white cat'?

You stress the need for economic, social and ecological balance. What are the main obstacles in the pursuit of this triple balance and how to overcome them?

Regional integration and international organizations

Considering such projects as the Trans-Pacific Partnership (TPP) and Transatlantic Trade and Investment Partnership (TTIP[1]), which process is of greater importance: globalization or regionalization?

Which of the initiatives is more important: TPP or BRI?

What is your opinion on the Asian Infrastructure Investment Bank (AIIB)?

What do you think about the 'New Silk Road Initiative'? What kind of problems will China face here?

There's talk of New Europe and Old Europe. Is there any financial or political barrier between these two groups of countries?

Political transformation and its results

What do you think about the 'Washington Consensus' and 'Shock Therapy'?

What shocks did 'New Europe' experience in the process of EU integration and what benefits did it reap?

How can the process of Polish economy transition be evaluated, and can it be considered finished?

What can China learn from the recent experience of Polish and CEE countries?

Has the Hungarian transformation process reversed course?

What has been the influence of Eastern European geopolitics on the economic and political development of the transitioning countries?

After the successful transformation, what changes can be expected in terms of the status of CEE countries on the international arena?

China

Is China a threat to the world?

On the one hand, it is often said that China will soon overtake the world's largest economy, but on the other hand there is much talk of the Chinese economy's weaknesses. How would you comment on that?

Will China overtake the United States and what would be the global consequences?

Will China be able to maintain a high economic growth rate over the next ten years?

How can China maintain its economic growth at a high rate, which would be good for China and the world alike?

Will the Chinese renminbi be included in the SDR[2] [Special Drawing Rights] basket of currencies? Is it important for China?

How can we solve the problem of the income gap in China? Is it possible?

Should corruption be considered as one of the most important problems in China?

What lesson can contemporary China learn from the experiences of small countries such as Poland or Singapore?

Europe and Poland

What is the current situation of CEE countries in terms of reindustrialization?

What is the state of the Polish middle class compared to the Chinese one, and what can be done to divide income in a more equitable way?

What is the share of wages in Poland's GDP?

How will Polish economic policy change due to the presidential and parliamentary elections?

How did the opening and liberalization of the financial system in Poland react after the financial crisis of 2008?

What is the impact on Poland's economy of the European and US sanctions imposed on Russia?

Trade relations with Poland and CEE

What is the current state of relations between China and CEE countries, and how will these relationships develop in the future?

How can the current development of trade cooperation between Poland and China be evaluated?

What will be the future of trade cooperation between Poland and China in the context of the new government in Poland?

Greece and Ukraine

What do you think about the present stage of the Greek crisis?

Should China be concerned about the problem of Greece?

Will Greece drop out of the eurozone?

What do you think about the crisis and conflict in Ukraine?

3. Chinese panoply of questions

The Chinese panoply of questions is indeed rich and comprehensive; colorful, one may say. The selection presented here is by no means a result of representative research; it's just a specific review of questions arising out of the interests of the students and professors I met. If these are some of the issues they ask about, then these are the topics they reflect on and discuss as they want to know more about what is happening in their backyard and elsewhere, and why. In particular, if it is or may be related to what is happening in China. Back there, they also know that he who asks is a fool for a moment, but he who doesn't ask remains a fool for ever.

It's good to realize at this point that there are a total of twenty-seven million students in China. This is more than the entire population of Romania and Slovakia combined. More than half a million (ca. 550,000) young Chinese are studying abroad. Not only to gain knowledge and professional skills, so needed in the dynamically developing economy, but also to better understand and communicate with others, as the Chinese emphasize themselves. A great majority of those studying abroad follow a course in the West; there are ca. 330,000 of them in the United States. Importantly, they are also quite curious, so every time I give lectures at US universities, I always have to answer their questions, too. They are active. But not all of them rush back to the homeland. Having obtained their degree, ca. 80 percent of them, now alumni, return to China.

To ensure the percentage of those coming back keeps rising, China is working toward encouraging the return of the most talented compatriots, who, right after graduation, receive lucrative job offers in the countries to which they went intending only to get a university education. In other words, China is combating the brain drain. If we assume that a full master's course in the United States takes five years and that this is the one chosen by the Chinese, ca. 65,000 people graduate every year. If one-fifth do not come back, it means that the US job market profits by absorbing ca. 13,000 young, well-educated, energetic and innovative employees every year. This has obvious benefits in terms of enriching US human capital, and an obvious cost for the Chinese economy and society, especially considering that most students from China pay for their education from their own pockets rather than US scholarship funding.

However, life itself raises so many doubts that from this perspective it seems to be a constant stream of questions and answers. No wonder, then, that what is clear from the students' questions is their quite significant knowledge on the one hand, and on the other, the genuine willingness to test and broaden it. No wonder, also, that – not only in China, as it is the case everywhere – many questions stem from the current narrative, especially from media accounts of what has happened here and there. When listening to students' questions, it is evident what books they read and which media they follow for current events, and based on what media their lecturers present to them their point of view, which is later internalized and treated as their own.

With respect to the economic issues discussed in the professional community, it is also important that theoretical knowledge is confronted with practical challenges. Unfortunately, the former often cannot keep up with the latter. However, the overall impression is that the lecturers' competence is high and they are well versed in the problematics discussed. Meanwhile, there is an awareness that an economist's answer is a question to a politician. Also in China. This is why, especially at universities, one can feel a lot of pressure to make both the economy and policies as knowledge-based as possible. And again, as is the case everywhere, while at universities this reliance on knowledge is believed to be far from the desired level, to political actors it seems sufficient. Well, sadly it is never and nowhere sufficient. Not even in China.

New Pragmatism with Chinese Characteristics

1. Vision rather than illusions

The Chinese leader Xi Jinping advocates globalization, which may increasingly aid the long-term development of the world economy. The US president Donald Trump does not serve globalization or even hinders the development of the world economy. Maybe some of his actions will revive the US economy in the short run, but they are harmful to the global economy. And later on, there will be a growing imbalance, including another budget deficit and public debt within the United States itself. It may seem to some that 'Trumponomics' is a present-day Reaganomics, but it's just an illusion. Thirty-five years ago, Reaganomics was the grist to the mill of neoliberalism, whose harmful effect is only fully visible *ex post*. The harmful effect of Trump's economic nationalism will also become increasingly clear with time.

While the multiyear 4 percent GDP growth is the US president's pipe dream, the New Silk Road is a realistic initiative of the Chinese president, incorporating his country even further than to date into the globalization process. At the same time, this is an attempt to make the process more inclusive. The US president harbors illusions, whereas the Chinese leader has a vision. Quite the opposite of the situation half a century ago. Such dissonance has colossal implications for the world's future.

It is quite typical that at the time the 45th president of the United States, during his inauguration on the steps of Capitol Hill, was saying (or actually shouting) 'America First!', at the World Economic Forum in Davos, the president of China was appealing for the defense of free trade, warning that there can be no winner in the trade war Trump threatened to wage. Let us go even further: since such a war has been already launched by the American president, which is accusing China of currency manipulations, and punitive, prohibitively high customs have been imposed on Chinese goods purchased by the United States, in the long-run China stands to lose less than the United States.

It is characteristic that when President Xi assures the French president Emmanuel Macron, in a phone conversation, that he will defend the Paris Agreement of December 2015, aimed at limiting climate change by controlling greenhouse gas emissions, President Trump maintains his unfortunate decision to pull the United States out from this agreement, reached with such difficulty and so badly needed.

Though certainly China will not become, by the end of the twenty-first century, a true 'middle country' as there will be no such thing in the world of the future, its economy, with a GDP at PPP of 21.3 trillion dollars, is already bigger than the US economy by nearly 15 percent (calculated at market exchange rates, the US GDP of 18.6 trillion dollars is 63 percent bigger than China's) and 11 percent bigger than that of the EU, still including the UK (calculated at market exchange rates, the EU's GDP of 16.3 trillion dollars is bigger than the Chinese one by nearly 43 percent). Let us not forget, however, that all this might comes not only from Shanghai or Shenzhen, as China still employs as many people (28.3 percent) in agriculture as in industry (29.3 percent of the workforce).[1]

Let us also bear in mind that China is the world's biggest exporter and second biggest importer after the United States. Beijing has amassed the world's largest foreign-exchange reserves, amounting to more than the sum total of reserves held by the four economies ranking after China on this list: Japan, Switzerland, Saudi Arabia and Taiwan. If we were to look far ahead into the future and see Chinese reserves together with those held by Taiwan and Hong Kong, the currency reserves of such 'greater' China exceed the sum total of the aforementioned countries plus those of Russia, India and South Korea.

Therefore, China has enough to maintain the stability of its own economy, and, at the same time, it has at its disposal immense capital to invest outside the country. It is already doing so, because, even though the cumulated foreign direct investment (FDI) in China amounts to 1.46 trillion dollars, and the Chinese FDI abroad to 1.29 trillion, the Chinese FDI in other countries has, since 2015, been higher than foreign investment in China. In 2016, Chinese FDI reached a historically high level of 189 billion dollars, as much as 40 percent more than a year before. Over 37 billion of this amount (as much as 77 percent more than in the previous year) went to EU member states. It's curious that while some seek – and rightly so – to attract Chinese capital, others accuse China of neocolonial aspirations. There is no threat of the latter as – let us reiterate – to Beijing, Chinese outward economic expansion is mostly an instrument of the policy that serves internal affairs.

At this stage of the reforms, it's a good way to ensure high economic growth and, consequently, the rising incomes of the population, and to hold in check the immense internal migration from the countryside to cities. It is worth adding that the fast income growth rate also helps maintain social order. When asked about this, Chinese economists reply that, if for no other reason, the likelihood of something akin to the Arab Spring, triggered by economic stagnation coupled with authoritarian regime, is next to zero.

While Americans save 17.6 percent of their national income (21.4 per cent in the EU), the value for China is as huge as 46 percent (*sic!*). This is too much and though China is slowly trying to reduce the propensity to save, favoring a relatively faster growth of consumer spending, the country still has huge funds for domestic and foreign investment. No wonder, then, that it is looking all over the world for attractive locations to place them. Striding the New Silk Road, China also reaches CEE, and this current will pick up speed with the BRI program is targeting also East Central European countries – from Estonia and Latvia in the north, through the Czech Republic and Slovakia in the middle, all the way to Albania and Macedonia in the south. Poland, the largest economy of the region, has absorbed, to date, less Chinese FDI than Romania and Hungary, but in 2016 the amount already stood at over half a billion dollars and, importantly, it keeps rising.

2. 16+1 initiative

When China enters the international arena, it does so with considerable flair. This is also the case with the New Silk Road. It is a mammoth program, one of the largest ever, targeting countries accounting for around two-fifths of global production and inhabited by nearly two-thirds of the world's population. In each of those countries, appetites have been whetted and their authorities expect a lot from it. Perhaps in some cases these expectations will be more than met, and surely others will be disappointed. Also, because the BRI is still in its initial phase, without well-developed segments, there are many uncertainties and a lack of concrete terms. Little wonder then that, for example in Poland, some have their eyes on the huge deals they hope to strike with the Chinese when building a central communication port for at least 10 billion dollars, with an enormous airport and multimodal dry port facilities. It is similar in other countries, though this is often wishful thinking that is not supported by real plans and the intentions of China itself.

Meanwhile, there is no shadow of doubt that China is very much interested in expanding the infrastructure necessary on the road to the wealthy European market, of which the catching-up Eastern European countries are also an inalienable part. Mindful, for political reasons, not to overlook any of them, and, at the same time, having little concern for the economies between the Baltic and the Adriatic (which are small from China's perspective), China lumped them all together, baptizing the whole lot '16'. Taking account of China itself, the program is known as the '16+1' initiative.

Well, not all of them, after all. Let us pass over the fact that the map features a bright spot in the Balkans, which is outside the 16+1, namely Kosovo. Its independence, declared in 2008, has not, to date,

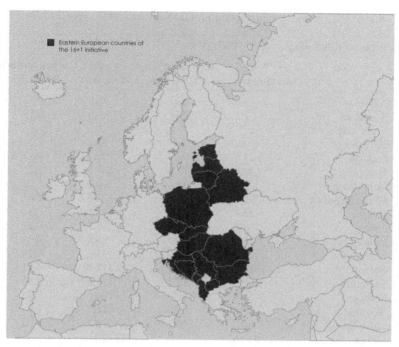

Eastern European countries of
the 16+1 initiative

Map 4 Eastern European countries of the 16+1 initiative
Source: Own compilation.

been recognized by China, or by Russia, another permanent member of the UN Security Council. This is mostly because it has not been acknowledged, either, by Serbia, which still considers Kosovo as an autonomous part of its own territory. The situation gets complicated as it's difficult to expect China to recognize Kosovo's sovereignty if Russia fails to do so, and it probably won't if the West fails to recognize the territorial integrity of Crimea and Russia, which does not seem likely for many, many years to come. Kosovo, however, due to its tiny size (GDP at PPP of only 19.4 billion dollars, representing 0.8 pro mille of China's GDP) is of relatively marginal economic importance. What matters is other Eastern European economies, though all of them, including the largest one, Poland, are dwarfed by the Chinese giant.

Table 6 GDP of sixteen CEE economies in comparison to China (2017)

Wyszczególnienia	PKB (KR)		PKB (PSN)	
	w mld dolarów	w procentach PKB Chin	w mld dolarów	w procentach PKB Chin
Albania	13.0	0.11	35.9	0.16
Bosnia & Hercegovina	17.5	0.15	43.9	0.19
Bulgaria	56.0	0.47	152.4	0.66
Croatia	53.5	0.45	100.2	0.43
Hungary	132.0	1.11	283.6	1.23
Montenegro	4.4	0.04	10.9	0.05
Czech Republic	209.7	1.76	372.6	1.61
Estonia	25.7	0.22	41.2	0.18
Latvia	30.2	0.25	53.5	0.23
Lithuania	46.7	0.39	90.6	0.39
Macedonia	11.4	0.10	31.6	0.14
Poland	510.0	4.27	1,111.0	4.81
Romania	204.9	1.72	474.0	2.05
Serbia	39.4	0.33	106.6	0.46
Slovakia	95.0	0.80	178.7	0.77
Slovenia	48.1	0.40	70.4	0.30
China	11,940.0		23,120.0	

Source: Own calculations based on World Bank data.
MR – market rate
PPP – purchasing power parity.

However, what cannot be passed over is that the map fails to include three other Eastern European countries: Belarus, Moldova and, importantly, Ukraine. The latter is not only the most populous country in this part of the continent, but also an important transit route from Asia to Western Europe. Logistics will often require transports of products carried through the territories of the former USSR from China to the West, and brought from there to China, to go through Ukraine. Of course, this can and certainly will happen, in justified cases, without formally including Ukraine (as well as Belarus and the relatively less significant Moldova) in the BRI project and turning its Eastern European part into the 19+1 initiative (or 20+1 with Kosovo). Geopolitics gets the upper hand also this time, because it's obvious that this part of post-Soviet Europe is still influenced by Russia and its views on various aspects of institutionalizing international economic cooperation. That's why it's possible to be an Eastern European country, but formally not to participate in an important infrastructure program that China offers to this part of the world.

Some take the opportunity to accuse China of using the 16+1 initiative to interfere with the European integration process. For now, eleven countries out of the sixteen are EU member states, and the remaining five may and should join it before the end of the next decade. The European Commission announced that the two Western Balkan countries that have made the most significant progress with reforms – Montenegro and Serbia – can become members of the grouping in 2025, but this should be seen either as a sign of incorrigible optimism, or a deliberate trick to mobilize them to harmonize their structures, institutions and standards with EU requirements more rapidly. Quite importantly and understandably, the European Commission, guided by its geopolitics, also mentions the sixth country of the region, Kosovo, which is overlooked by China due to its own geopolitics.

Hence, the rhetoric accompanying the publication of the European Commission's 'Strategy for the Western Balkans' (European Commission 2018) in early 2018, maintaining that China's economic activity in the Balkans is a cause for concern, comes as a surprise. If China, understandably guided by its strategic interests, will contribute, if only slightly, to improving and developing the floundering quality of the transport, transit and transshipment infrastructure in the Eastern European economies, this will be conducive rather than harmful to deepening and broadening European integration.

China's increasing presence in Europe should not be feared; it should be skillfully taken advantage of. If China wants to implement its *win-win* strategy here as well, we should applaud it, but without going too far. Unlike some politicians and officials in Brussels, the foreign minister of Hungary, Peter Szijjarto, when welcoming to Budapest the Chinese prime minister, Li Keqiang, arriving for a 16+1 summit in November 2017, said: 'We, in this region, have looked at China's leading role in the new world order as an opportunity rather than a threat' (Peto 2017). He is right and shows political courage as a foreign minister of an EU and NATO member state, as this stance is quite different to that displayed both by some Eurocrats and, most of all, by the new 'big brother' from across the ocean.

First and foremost, though, one has to do the math as this is not a matter of sentiment; an economic calculation is what counts here. This is also the case with the first major infrastructure project carried out by China in CEE – a 336-kilometer railway line from Belgrade to Budapest (184 kilometers in Serbia and 152 in Hungary). The cost of the project is ca. 3 billion dollars, with its Hungarian part to be funded by Hungarians in 85 percent with a soft loan, at a below-market interest rate, provided by China Exim Bank. This project, to be carried out mostly by Chinese companies, will not only halve the travel time between the capital cities of Serbia and Hungary, as trains are expected to zoom at 160–200 kilometers per hour, but, most of all, provide an overland route for commodity freight from the port of Piraeus (Greek but owned by the Chinese, as we already know) to Eastern Europe and further. To make it happen, the railway route from Greece (which is in the EU) through Macedonia and part of Serbia (which are not in the EU yet) needs to be modernized, but all in good time.

3. China coming to our rescue?

In the same way as a quarter of a century ago, with Cold War One coming to an end following the collapse of the Soviet Union, it was naive to expect that the United States, taking advantage of its economic power, including financial, political and military might, would 'save the world' and effectively become its progressive leader (Brzeziński 2007), it would be equally naive at present to expect something similar from China. Despite its might, it has neither the funds nor – unlike the United States – the intentions to do so, the way it is suspected of by some and accused of by others. China by no means wishes to dominate the world, it just wants to use globalization to its advantage, not necessarily at the expense of others, and sometimes even helping them, too. If that proved to be the case, if not the whole world, then at least its major part could possibly be put on the right track rather than trudging along back roads.

Some expect a lot – possibly too much – from the BRI and its regional versions, such as 16+1, while others fear becoming dependent on China. Some, especially naive politicians, of whom, sadly, there is no shortage in any country, unrealistically assume that China will help them solve their domestic problems, while others warn not to fall into the trap of overcommitting to China this time. Some have an increasingly favorable opinion of the Chinese and are fond of them; others, however, remain less convinced and have no liking for them. A number of factors can be seen to play out in these opinions: resentments rooted in the past, experience of close proximity, authentic economic aid, promises for the future. And they also reveal the effect of the opinion-leading media,

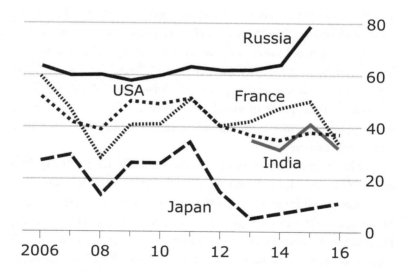

Diagram 15 Who likes China? Percentage of people expressing a favorable opinion about China

Source: Own compilation based on the results of a poll by the Pew Research Center.

which hardly anywhere (if at all) sympathize with China more than it deserves. It's the other way round.

It is striking how these factors commingle to shape public opinion. Let us remember that the polls, to whose results we refer, are representative. It also means that those answering the question on whether they have a favorable or negative opinion of China, in a large majority of cases, have never been to the Middle Country. Their views are shaped, to an overwhelming extent, by the public narrative, with the media leading the way, and they are always more or less influenced by politics. This explains – in addition to an awareness of history and geoeconomics – how it's possible that as many as eight out of ten Russians have a positive opinion of their southern neighbor, while only one in ten Japanese people has a favorable view of their western neighbor. If we take a closer look at what lies beneath these generalized averages, in each of the above countries relatively the most positive views are held by young people, aged 20–29, with the middle-aged (30–49) being more skeptical, and dislike being manifested more strongly among the older generation, aged over 50. In the United States and Japan, those thinking well of China are twice as numerous among young people as among the older age group. History definitely left its imprint on such opinions; people of different ages had different experiences. Will the former not be disillusioned and will the latter 'rejuvenate' their point of view? Or maybe the former are in for a disappointment and will join the older respondents, who treat China with more reserve?

Unlike in nature, in politics and the economy no system is pure as we are always dealing with some sort of mixture of the two. This, as we know well by now, is also the case with China, where elements of a communist centrally planned economy, not yet fully removed, interplay with elements of an open free market economy; where still significant symptoms of statism coexist with liberalized capitalist entrepreneurship. It is very important that China of all places – the country that means so much to the future of the world – is where new pragmatism is coming to the fore.

Advocating globalization while pointing out the imperative to make it more inclusive, realizing the absolute need to decrease the scale of trade and financial imbalance in the global economy, taking even greater care of the environmental balance than some highly developed countries (having, in the past, contributed a lot to upsetting it), China is slowly entering the path of economic policy suggested by new pragmatism. Neoliberalism hardly exists there, a corrupted state capitalism is increasingly fading (though it is still too prevalent), while more and more new pragmatism ideas are gaining ground (Hu 2018). Indeed, nobody else, on such a great scale and with such global consequences, can equally effectively couple the power of the invisible hand of the market with the power of the visible hand of the state. Only Nordic economies do it better, also Canada, but their impact on the processes taking place in the global economy is marginal.

A great battle to streamline globalization is on. This – coupled with security issues and concern for the environment – may determine the 'to be or not to be' of our civilization. China can significantly help co-shape the desirable face of the future, limiting the mounting global threats and the risk of a great disaster that goes far beyond the economic dimension. And this is what the world is in for if, on the one hand, the economy is switched back to the neoliberal *business as usual* groove, and, on the other hand, if we fail to control the escalation of new nationalism. However, we can hope that neither of the two happens, and the credit for that should go, to a great extent, to China.

If China manages to defend free trade from the designs of economic nationalists, if it saves the Paris Agreement on counteracting global warming, and talks the United States out of its reprehensible intention to leave this project; if, by investing trillions of US dollars in the coming decades in Africa and the Middle East, it stimulates a high growth rate there, which, by improving living conditions and slowing down the demographic explosion, will save Europe from the influx of tens of millions of immigrants; if it helps find a solution to the festering conflict around North Korea's nuclear program, the way it helped with Iran, then we will all benefit from it.

There are more of those 'ifs'. The greatest of them all is a warning that if China fails to cope with the demographic syndrome – if it fails to wisely overcome it by using threefold measures in the areas of population policy, controlled migration and technologies replacing human work – the challenges resulting from an unavoidably aging society will halt its daring march along the path of economic development. Then the country will be stuck somewhere on the way toward realizing the bold and optimistic plan to build by the mid-twenty-first century a 'great modern socialist country that is prosperous, strong, democratic, culturally advanced, harmonious and beautiful'.

This plan will remain just a plan, if – and this is the second great 'if' – China fails to significantly reduce the scale of income and wealth inequalities by means of threefold measures in the areas of education, regional development and budget transfers. Currently, inequalities are the cost of the economic success achieved, but with such a burden it's impossible to keep increasing production without social disturbances, so entering a multiyear path of income inequality reduction is an imperative for future development.

It can be a beautiful country, where the water is clean and the grass is green, which gladdens the residents' eyes with the beauty of unpolluted nature. So, if China wishes to be beautiful, while being utterly overcrowded, it must show yet greater determination about environmental protection and strive for ecological balance. It is already doing a lot about it, but if it doesn't do much more – and this is the third great 'if' – then it will prove to itself and others that one cannot be dirty and beautiful at the same time.

Last but not least, there will be no harmony and beauty if – and this is the fourth great 'if'– on a tide of its immense economic achievements and efforts to strengthen its global economic position, it yields to the temptation of pursuing an aggressive international policy and tries to impose this model on others or gets drawn into foreign conflicts.

In long-term economic processes, a solution to some problems always involves generating new ones. It's no different in the contemporary world, including such an important part of it that is China. It will be no different also in the future. With some difficulties overcome, others will crop up. The current balance of costs incurred and benefits obtained in the social economic process in the Middle Country is clearly positive. The Chinese build their optimism on their conviction that this will continue. Furthermore, they manage to export some of this optimism in these unstable and uncertain times, as they are happy to share it.

China will not convert Eurasia into Asiope, but it will irreversibly change the geopolitical and geoeconomic structures and importance of the continents stretching from the north Pacific to the north Atlantic.

China should not be feared, it should be counted on. It will not save the world but it can help prevent it from turning upside down.

Final Reflections

Since history is not over, and the West is coping poorly with the imperative to ensure existential rationality, then maybe we should pin our hopes on the East? Allegedly, we have only a hundred years left before, in the early twenty-second century, it dominates the world, but it would be better if none of the four corners of the world was dominant; after all, it's round. There is nothing better than harmony, equilibrium, balance, healthy proportions. To allow them to take root, it is necessary to be guided by a different system of values than before, one that does not overlook true solidarity and shared responsibility. Can humanity approach it, being eight billion strong in a few years, and ten billion strong in several decades, if it has failed to achieve it when it was just one billion strong two centuries ago and two billion strong a century ago?[1]

There is an opportunity to deepen globalization provided that it is given a more reasonable, inclusive dimension. Ironically, to an economist, this opportunity does not stem from economic logic, but from political circumstances on the macro scale and psychological ones with respect to human beings. They find it easiest to unite in a communal effort when there's an enemy to confront. Some are clearly in search of an enemy. It's not much of a problem if these are individuals or small social groups; it becomes more serious if these are large countries. Some of them look for such an external enemy by creating it with its own politics and the rhetoric of its leaders. It's alarming that the United States wishes to make China its foe, which is directly announced by its president on Twitter. It is reassuring that China does not wish to turn other countries into foes and looks instead for further and further channels for cooperation. It's astounding, but China seems to better understand what's at stake at the current civilizational crossroads.

Once, a long time ago, *Pax Romana* reigned across the Mediterranean civilization. Not for ever. Once, not so long ago, *Pax Americana* was to reign all over the world. This illusion was very short-lived. Now, some fear and other delude themselves that *Pax Sinica* is coming. No, it's not, but we can pin some hopes on the fact that with China's inevitably growing role in the global political and economic playfield, with time, the country will be able to transmit to the rest of the world at least some of its capacity for collective actions, for community behaviors, without which humanity will not manage itself.

If civilization is to survive in relative peace and calm, realistically this can only be based on a social market economy. As a matter of fact, it's hard to imagine that another political system could assure worldwide existential rationality. It would be great if the Scandinavian-type social market economies emanated to the whole world, leaving an axiological and institutional mark, but it's a pipe dream for the majority of regions. Meanwhile, if China sets the course for that very system – again, obviously, with Chinese characteristics – this may both greatly contribute to the welfare of its society and give a lot of hints to others.

We need to become integrated, be community-minded in our thoughts and actions, on a large, supranational or even global scale, as the enemy is there. Barbarians are already at the gate, but this time they are not other nations or states with their armies, nearer or more faraway neighbors with their bad intentions. The Earth and humanity are not threatened by external foes as we do not have them; what we have is worldwide challenges. And that is the enemy we need to take on. We need to get organized and defend ourselves against global warming and environmental devastation; together, because separately it's no longer possible. We need to join forces to manage demographic processes in the long run; otherwise in certain regions of the world people will be helpless as there will be too many of them, while elsewhere they will be not able to cope with the challenges because there will be too few of them. We need to manage the broadly defined economic exchange, now irrevocably a globalized one, in a different way than in the past, in order to alleviate conflict-conducive income and wealth inequalities.

All this should happen within the framework of institutional order rather than amid chaotic mess. How to organize this order effectively? It also requires some functional form of leadership. How to appoint it? This requires a brand new perspective on the problems we are confronted with. How to solve them? Now, we need to look for ways to subordinate not only particular interests to social ones, and, mind you, even in this respect not much has been achieved yet, but also to subordinate national interests to global ones. Is that utopia? It is for now, but there is still the future.

Notes

Chapter 1

1   Quote from Twitter, @realDonaldTrump, 11:50, 2 March 2018.

2   Quote from Twitter, @realDonaldTrump, 09:43, 3 March 2018.

3   China, sadly, also restrictively limits access to Western social networking forums on its territory, but at least it offers its own Weibo, Baidu and WeChat instead, and the Alibaba platform for shopping.

4   Both the structure and level of currency reserves change over time. The Chinese reserves, worth the equivalent of ca. 3.2 trillion dollars, represent the balance as at the beginning of 2018. They reached a peak level – nearly 4 trillion dollars – in June 2014.

Chapter 2

1   The population of the Middle East is estimated at ca. 450 million, as this part of the world also includes the essentially African Egypt, with a population of 97 million (geographically Asian Sinai is inhabited by ca. 1.4 million people), and Cyprus, with a population of merely 1.2 million. Without those two countries, the Middle East – geographically situated in Asia except for the tiny European fragment of Turkey of 23,764 square kilometers – has ca. 350 million people. This is the sum total of the populations of Bahrain, Iraq, Iran, Israel, Jordan, Kuwait, Lebanon, Oman, Palestine, Qatar, Saudi Arabia, Syria, Turkey, United Arab Emirates and Yemen.

2   Member states of ASEAN (Association of South East Asian Nations) are Brunei, the Philippines, Indonesia, Cambodia, Laos, Malaysia, Myanmar, Singapore, Thailand and Vietnam. The grouping is inhabited by ca. 650 million people (8.7 percent of humanity) and produces ca. 10.5 percent of GWP (at purchasing power parity, PPP).

3   Member states of SAARC (South Asian Association for Regional Cooperation) are Afghanistan, Bangladesh, Bhutan, India, Nepal,

Maldives, Pakistan and Sri Lanka. These countries are inhabited by
ca. 1,770 million people (nearly 24 percent of humanity), who produce
ca. 13.7 percent of GWP (at PPP).

4 The remaining countries with a population of more than 100 million
are – ordered by the population size – United States (327 million), Brazil
(208), Nigeria (191), Russia (143), Mexico (125) and Ethiopia (196). Soon
this group of non-Asian countries with such a large population will be
joined by Egypt.

5 Six centuries ago, the Xuande emperor, who ruled China from 1426
to 1435, put an end to the period of great voyages to the northern basins
of the Indian Ocean, Persian Gulf and Arabian and Red Sea. Expeditions
led by admiral Zheng He were important to Beijing not only in military
terms; most of all they were of substantial economic significance as they
fostered trade. Actually, the father of the emperor, the Hongxi emperor,
on the throne only for two years (1424–1425), had already blocked those
maritime escapades, choosing an inward orientation and opting out
of expansion in South East Asia and in the eastern borders of Africa.
Nobody and nothing – except for individual preferences – forced them
to take this incomprehensible about-face. Four hundred years later, or
two centuries ago, China was again shutting itself away, though under
quite different circumstances, because at the same time it was increasingly
penetrated by Western imperialism.

6 Similar processes are taking place in other parts of the world, also in post-
socialist Eastern European economies, the most advanced of which are
increasingly unable to compete on the basis of low wages. For example,
in Poland in December 2017, the average gross monthly salary in the
business enterprise sector fluctuated around 1,450 dollars, at the current
exchange rate, which exhibited a strong appreciation at the time. These
data relate to companies with more than nine employees, so the relevant
amount for the economy as a whole can be up to several hundred dollars
lower.

7 It's another paradox that it was the pressure from the West, especially
from the so-called troika (i.e. the European Commission, European
Central Bank and IMF), on Greece to improve its fiscal situation also
by privatizing state assets (Kolodko 2016) that made the government
in Athens sell the port of Piraeus. The investor was China's COSCO
Shipping Corporation.

8　　S&P 500 is a stock market index managed by Standard & Poor's, whose value is determined by New York Stock Exchange and NASDAQ prices for 500 companies with the largest market capitalization, mostly US ones.

9　　In the case of Poland, the reality is that at a market exchange rate of 3.4 zlotys per dollar in early 2018, it was worth, at PPP, ca. 1.56 zlotys. In other words, 1,560 zlotys can buy in Poland as much as 1,000 dollars can in the United States.

10　Brexit will have the opposite and slightly stronger effect on the value of the grouping's aggregate GDP than the EU accession of the first round of post-socialist economies in 2004. This will happen because the UK, generating a GDP at PPP of ca. 2.9 trillion dollars, contributes to GWP 2.3 percent of its value.

11　In recent years, the Indian population has been growing ca. three times faster than that of China; by 1.17 and 0.41 percent, respectively.

12　Later on, the letter S was added and BRIC turned into BRICS, as the South African Republic was included in this figure. In addition to geoeconomic and political arguments (it's good to have someone from Africa), the alphabet was a deciding factor as adding, say, N for Nigeria, which is a larger economy than South Africa, did not seem suitable to the authors. Taking Indonesia or Pakistan was not feasible either because BRICS sounds better than BRICN, BRICJ or BRICP …

13　The power of the compound interest means that an annual average 7.2 percent growth continuing over ten years is enough for any given value to double.

Chapter 3

1　　By way of comparison, in Poland the population growth rate in 2017 was negative, standing at -0.13 percent, while in the EU, it stood at 0.23. It amounted to 0.81 in the United States, and 1.06 percent worldwide.

2　　By way of comparison, total fertility rate in Poland decreased in the last half-century from 2.33 children per woman in 1967 to 1.35 in 2017.

3　　Data as per Worldometers statistics, available at http://www.worldometers.info/world-population/#.

4   *The World Economic Factbook* is a good source of comparative economic and demographic data, as well as selected information on religions and languages, geography and military matters, telecommunications and transport. It is published online by the US Central Intelligence Agency. It seems sometimes espionage organizations can do a good service to us all.

5   According to Polish Central Statistical Office data, the Chinese spend the most of all foreign tourists visiting Poland. In 2017, their spending stood at over 7,800 zlotys (ca. 2,200 dollars) per visitor. This is more or less as much as a two-person household spends in a whole month.

6   I first pointed out this 'injustice' a couple of years ago, when publishing in *The Economist* a commentary under the telling title 'Bring Poland to the G20, and Don't Cry for Argentina' (Kolodko 2014b).

7   In 2017, a not very successful G20 summit was held in Hamburg. A nice touch was the Chinese leader Xi Jinping offering a couple of cute giant pandas, Jiao Ping and Meng Meng, to the German chancellor Angela Merkel. This is also politics. Certainly more classy than the US president referring to China as its rival.

8   In March 1969, an acute Sino-Soviet conflict erupted on the Ussuri River, bordering the two countries, and escalated into an exchange of fire on Damansky Island. Several hundred soldiers died on both sides as a result of the shooting. It's unclear how many exactly, as each side overstated the enemy's casualties and understated its own. The battle of 15 March claimed 100 Chinese people and 250 Russians, according to the Chinese, and 27 Russians and 800 Chinese, according to the Russians.

Chapter 4

1   Eleven CEE post-socialist countries are now members of the EU. The EU was joined first by the Czech Republic, Estonia, Hungary, Latvia, Lithuania, Poland, Slovakia and Slovenia in 2004, then by Bulgaria and Romania in 2007, and finally by Croatia in 2013.

2   The most often used metric in this respect, the Gini index, which theoretically ranges from zero (when everyone gets the same share of income) to 1 (when somebody takes over the whole income) stands at ca. 0.4 in the United States, whereas in China it is around 0.46.

3   Shortages occurred exceptionally also in capitalist countries, including
     the United States and Japan, and especially in Great Britain during the
     Second World War, which were caused by the administrative measures
     adopted to suppress the inflationary price rises (Charlesworth 1956).
     This was accompanied by vast rationing schemes for goods in short
     supply. On a lesser scale, shortages also appeared after the 1973 oil crisis,
     when in the United States at times it was impossible to tank up a car due
     to the short supply of fuel on the market.

4   In Poland in mid-1989, about half of the prices, in terms of market value,
     were already deregulated. In countries such as Albania or Romania at
     that time, free market prices were almost non-existent.

5   I mean prices in the strict sense (i.e. the monetary expression of the value
     of consumer products and services exchanged on the market) rather than
     prices in the broad sense, also inclusive of the price of labor, i.e. wages,
     and the price of money in the future – namely, the interest rate – and the
     price of foreign currency – that is, the exchange rate.

6   Today, it can be observed in its extreme case in North Korea, on a lesser
     scale in Cuba, as well as, temporarily, in Venezuela and Zimbabwe.

7   In Poland, in the face of an unemployment rate in the order
     of 6–7 percent, or exceeding a million people in absolute numbers,
     we can hear that it's only natural unemployment, so no need to worry.
     Lobbyists for capitalist organizations, who like to call themselves
     employers, even claim there is actually no unemployment, forgetting
     that those one million people genuinely have no job and are looking for
     work. That's how the number of unemployed is defined and measured: as
     people with no job who are actively looking for employment.

8   It's worth recalling that the authors of the infamous shock without therapy
     in Poland at the turn of the 1990s announced that unemployment would
     amount 'only' to 400,000, and then – allegedly, after one year's moderate
     recession with a 3.1 percent GDP decline – it was supposed to stabilize
     or even go down. Such unrealistic assumptions were rightly criticized
     (Frydman, Kolodko and Wellisz 1991). What happened in reality was
     that unemployment grew for five years, exceeding three million, i.e.
     over 18 percent in 1994 (Kolodko and Nuti 1997).

9   The official unemployment rate in China is 4 percent but it is certainly
     higher as a lot of those migrating from the countryside to cities don't
     find work but are not registered as unemployed. Thus, they are not

included in the official statistics. In early March 2018, Prime Minister Li Keqiang, during a session of the National People's Congress (Chinese parliament) presented the government's economic policy goals, one of which, for the first time ever, was to keep urban unemployment rate within 5.5 percent.

10 In the West, both in professional literature and in political commentaries, China is still nonsensically referred to as a communist country. This error stems from the practice of equating a single-party system with a communist state, and a dominant role of the state sector with a communist economy.

11 It's interesting that all those countries are monarchies, closer to the absolutist than the constitutional type. Also, other monarchies in the Arab world – from Jordan in the Middle East to Morocco in North West Africa – are doing better than republics.

12 Ponzi, though the name may sound Chinese to some people, was an Italian, Carlo Pietro Giovanni Ponzi, who created the first major financial pyramid one hundred years ago in Boston. With losses of 15 million dollars, it collapsed in 1920, with its architect going to jail for three and a half years. Prison failed to rehabilitate Ponzi: once released, he built a new pyramid, for which fraud he spent a further ten years in prison (Zuckoff 2006).

13 Justin Yifu Lin, a professor at Peking University, and senior vice president and chief economist of the World Bank from 2008 to 2012, was, from 2006 to 2010, a member of the Scientific Advisory Board at the TIGER Center for Transformation, Integration, and Globalization Economic Research (www.tiger.edu.pl), which I head at Kozminski University in Warsaw.

Chapter 5

1 It's interesting that Oxford University Press, on the cover of a book entitled *A Brief History of Neoliberalism* (Harvey 2005), placed photos of Ronald Reagan, Deng Xiaoping, Augusto Pinochet and Margaret Thatcher.

2 ABBC News commentator points out: 'There are also plenty of targeted provisions buried in the bill. Racehorse owners, motorsport speedway operators, theatrical productions and rum importers all get a late Christmas present' (Zurcher 2018).

3 For comparison's sake, the US public debt is nearly twice as high as the Chinese GDP (at market exchange rate).

Chapter 6

1   TTIP is a trade agreement whose main goal is to create an enormous
     free trade area encompassing the EU and the United States. It has been
     negotiated since 2013, but with Donald Trump as the US president,
     advocating protectionism rather than free trade, the project as originally
     conceptualized hangs in the balance.

2   Special Drawing Rights, the so-called paper gold, is an international
     cashless unit of account used by the IMF. SDRs mostly serve to settle
     respective countries' payment obligations to improve their balance of
     payments (IMF 2011). Chinese currency, the renminbi (or yuan, as it
     is commonly known), became part of the SDR basket in 2016 and its
     weight in this system for 2016–2020 was set at 10.9 percent. For the
     remaining currencies, the value is 41.7 percent for the US dollar, 30.9 for
     the euro, 8.3 for the Japanese yen and 8.1 percent for the pound sterling.
     It's worth adding that the renminbi's inclusion in the SDR system was
     mainly at the expense of the euro, whose share of the currency basket
     was reduced by 6.5 percentage points (between 2011 and 2015 it stood
     at 37.4 percent).

Chapter 7

1   For comparison's sake, the United States employs in agriculture, forestry
     and fisheries merely 0.7 percent of its workforce; 20.3 percent of
     employees work in industry and as many as 79 percent work in services.

Final Reflections

1   According to our best knowledge, humanity was one billion strong
     in 1804, and two billion strong in 1930. Since then, it first doubled its size
     by 1974, and it will double again by 2023, reaching eight billion. Such
     doubling has never before been possible nor will it be possible ever again.
     There will be ten billion of us, according to the current UN forecasts, as
     soon as in 2055. Soon …

References

Acemoglu, Daron and James A. Robinson (2012). *Why Nations Fail. The Origins of Power, Prosperity, and Poverty*, Crown Business, New York.

Ahuja, Ashvin, Nigel Chalk, Malhar Nabar, Papa N'Diaye and Nathan Porter (2012). 'An End to China's Imbalances?', IMF Working Paper, WP/12/100, International Monetary Fund, Washington, DC.

Andelman, David (2017). 'Trump's Biggest Nightmare? China and Russia's Newfound Friendship', CNN, 1 August (https://edition.cnn.com/2017/08/01/opinions/china-and-russia-are-teaming-up-andelman-opinion/index.html).

Anderson, Jon Lee (2017). 'Accelerating Revolution', *The New Yorker*, 8 December, pp. 42–53.

Bałtowski, Maciej (2017). 'Evolution of Economics and the New Pragmatism of Grzegorz W. Kolodko', TIGER Working Papers, No. 136 (http://www.tiger.edu.pl/Baltowski_Evolution%20of%20economics%20and%20the%20new%20pragmatism%20of%20Grzegorz%20W.%20Kolodko_III%202017.pdf).

Bauer, Tamás (1978). 'Investment Cycles in Planned Economies', *Acta Oeconomica*, Vol. 21, No. 3, pp. 243–260.

BBC (2018a). 'CIA Chief Says China "as big a threat to US" as Russia', BBC News, 30 January (http://www.bbc.com/news/world-us-canada-42867076).

BBC (2018b). 'US Senate Reaches Two-Year Budget Deal' [2018], BBC News, February 7. (http://www.bbc.com/news/world-us-canada-42981072).

BBC (2018c). 'Trump Steel Tariffs: Trade Wars Are Good, Says Trump', BBC News, 2 March (http://www.bbc.com/news/world-us-canada-43257712).

BBC (2018d). 'Rex Tillerson Slams China's Relationship with Africa', BBC News, 5 March (http://www.bbc.com/news/world-us-canada-43307461).

BBC (2018e). 'Trump blocks Broadcom's bid for Qualcomm on security grounds', BBC News, 13 March (http://www.bbc.com/news/business-43380893).

BBC (2018f). 'Xi Jinping Warns Any Attempt to Split China is "doomed to fail"', BBC News, 20 March (http://www.bbc.com/news/world-asia-china-43466685).

Bell, Daniel A. (2015). *The China Model: Political Meritocracy and the Limits of Democracy*, Princeton University Press, Princeton, NJ.

Berger, Ron, Chong Ju Cho and Ram Herstein (2013). 'China's Social Market Economy: The Leverage of Economic Growth', *International Journal of Asian Business and Information Management*, Vol. 4, No. 1, pp. 21–30.

Bershidsky, Leonid (2017). 'Russia's Military Is Leaner, but Meaner', Bloomberg View, 14 December (https://www.bloomberg.com/view/articles/2017-12-14/russia-s-military-is-leaner-but-meaner).

Berthold, Rolf (2017). 'About the 19th National Congress of the CPC', *China Today*, November, pp. 30–31.

Block, Fred. (1994). 'The Roles of the State in the Economy', in Niel J. Smelser and Richard Swedberg (eds.), *The Handbook of Economic Sociology*, Princeton University Press, Princeton, NJ.

Bolt, Andrew (2017). 'Turkey Threatens to Drown Europe in Muslims', *Herald Sun*, 17 March (http://www.heraldsun.com.au/blogs/andrew-bolt/turkey-threatens-to-drown-europe-in-muslims/news-story/909cba32fe5e8e1b029eac518fd3d71a).

Bremmer, Ian (2010). *The End of the Free Market. Who Wins the War Between States and Corporations?*, Portfolio, New York.

Brzeziński, Zbigniew (2007). *Second Chance: Three Presidents and the Crisis of American Superpower*, Basic Books, New York.

Buc, Hernán Büchi (2006). 'How Chile Successfully Transformed Its Economy', Backgrounder, No. 1958, 18 September, Heritage Foundation, Washington, DC (https://www.semanticscholar.org/paper/How-Chile-Successfully-Transformed-Its-Economy-Buc/a74e75a974df8de54872aeaf8fe71207e6c337b8).

Bulletin (2018). 'A New Abnormal: It Is *Still* 2 Minutes to Midnight', *Bulletin of the Atomic Scientists*, University of Chicago, 25 January (https://thebulletin.org/clock/2018).

Charlesworth, Harold K. (1956). *The Economics of Repressed Inflation*, Routledge, Abingdon.

Cheremukhin, Anton, Mikhail Golosov, Sergei Guriev and Aleh Tsyvinski (2015). 'The Economy of People's Republic of China from 1953', NBER Working Paper, No. 21397, July.

China Daily (2017a). 'China's Private Sector Regains Strength on Optimistic Economic Outlook', *China Daily*, 2 August (http://www.chinadaily.com.cn/business/2017-08/02/content_30328022.htm).

China Daily (2017b). 'Xi Jinping and His Era', *China Daily*, 18–19 November, pp. 5–8.

Cieślik, Jerzy (2016). *Entrepreneurship in Emerging Economies: Enhancing Its Contribution to Socio-Economic Development*, Palgrave Macmillan, Basingstoke.

Csaba, László (2009). *Crisis in Economics?*, Akadémiai Kiadó, Budapest.

Dickens, Charles (2006). *Oliver Twist*, Sterling Publishing, New York.

Easterly, William (2002). *The Elusive Quest for Growth. Economists' Adventures and Misadventures in the Tropics*, MIT Press, Cambridge, MA.

Easterly, William (2006). *White Man's Burden: Why the West's Efforts to Aid the Rest Have Done So Much Ill and So Little Good*, Penguin, New York.

Economist (2012a). 'Teenage Angst', *The Economist*, 25 August (http://www.economist.com/node/21560890).

Economist (2013). 'The Sinodependency Index. Middling Kingdom', *The Economist*, 17 July (https://www.economist.com/blogs/graphicdetail/2013/07/sinodependency-index).

Economist (2016). 'The New Nationalism', *The Economist*, 19 November (https://www.economist.com/news/leaders/21710249-his-call-put-america-first-donald-trump-latest-recruit-dangerous).

Economist (2018a). 'The Growing Danger of Great-Power Conflict. How Shifts in Technology and Geopolitics Are Renewing the Threat', *The Economist*, 25 January (https://www.economist.com/news/leaders/21735586-how-shifts-technology-and-geopolitics-are-renewing-threat-growing-danger).

Economist (2018b). 'China Moves into Latin America', *The Economist*, 3 February (https://www.economist.com/news/americas/21736192-asian-giant-taking-advantage-other-powers-lack-interest-region-china-moves)

Economist (2018c). 'How Does Chinese Tech Stack Up Against American Tech?', *The Economist*, 15 February (https://www.economist.com/news/americas/21736192-asian-giant-taking-advantage-other-powers-lack-interest-region-china-moves)

Economist (2018d). 'How the West Got China Wrong', *The Economist*, 1 March (https://www.economist.com/news/leaders/21737517-it-bet-china-would-head-towards-democracy-and-market-economy-gamble-has-failed-how).

Eichengreen, Barry, Donghyun Park and Kwanho Shin (2011). 'When Fast Growing Economies Slow Down: International Evidence and Implications for China', NBER Working Paper Series, Working Paper 16919, National Bureau of Economic Research, Washington, DC.

Emerging Europe (2017), 'Poland to Switch from Emerging to Developed Market', Emerging Europe, 16 October (http://emerging-europe.com/regions/poland/poland-switch-emerging-developed-market-september-2018/).

European Commission (2018). 'Strategy for the Western Balkans: EU Sets Out New Flagship Initiatives and Support for the Reform-Driven Region', European Commission, Strasbourg, 6 February (http://europa.eu/rapid/press-release_IP-18-561_en.htm).

Fisher, Irving (1973). '"I Discovered the Phillips Curve": A Statistical Relation Between Unemployment and Price Changes', *Journal of Political Economy*, Vol. 81, No. 2, pp. 496–502.

Fortune Global 500 (various years). 'CNN Money', *Fortune*.

Friedman, Thomas L. (2005). *The World Is Flat: A Brief History of the Twenty-First Century*, Farrar, Straus and Giroux, New York.

Frydman, Roman, Grzegorz W. Kolodko and Stanislaw Wellisz (1991). 'Stabilization Policies in Poland: A Progress Report', in Emil-Maria Claassen (ed.), *Exchange Rate Policies in Developing and Post-Socialist Countries*, An International Center for Economic Growth Publication, ICS Press, San Francisco, pp. 89–115.

Fukuyama, Francis (1989). 'The End of History', *The National Interest*, No. 16, Summer, pp. 3–18 (http://www.wesjones.com/eoh.htm).

Galbraith, James K. (2014). *The End of Normal: The Great Crisis and the Future of Growth*, Simon & Schuster, New York.

Galbraith, James K. (2018). 'Backwater Economics and New Pragmatism: Crises and Evolution of Economics', TIGER Working Papers Series, No. 138, Kozminski University, Warsaw (http://www.tiger.edu.pl/TWP%20No.%20138%20--%20Galbraith.pdf).

Haberler, Gottfried (1977). *Stagflation: An Analysis of Its Causes and Cures*, American Enterprise Institute for Public Policy Research, No. 329, Washington, DC.

Halper, Stefan (2010). 'The Beijing Consensus: How China's Authoritarian Model Will Dominate the Twenty-First Century', Basic Books, New York.

Harvey, David (2005). *A Brief History of Neoliberalism*, Oxford University Press, Oxford.

Hegel, Georg Wilhelm Friedrich (1956). *The Philosophy of History*, Dover Publications, Mineola, NY.

Heilbroner Robert and William Milberg (1995). *The Crisis of Vision in Modern Economic Thought*, Cambridge University Press, New York.

Hofman, Bert (2018). 'Reflections on Forty Years of China's Reforms', *East Asia & Pacific on the Rise* [blog], The World Bank, 1 February (https://blogs.worldbank.org/eastasiapacific/reflections-on-forty-years-of-china-reforms).

Hu, Biliang (2018). 'The Belt and Road Initiative and the Transformation of Globalization', Distinguished Lectures Series, Kozminski University, No. 26 (http://www.tiger.edu.pl/publikacje/dist.htm).

Huang, Yukon (2017). 'Cracking the China Conundrum: Why Conventional Economic Wisdom Is Wrong', Oxford University Press, New York.

Huntington, Samuel P. (1996). *The Clash of Civilizations and the Remaking of World Order*, Touchstone, New York.

IMF (2011). *Enhancing International Monetary Stability. A Role for the SDR?*, International Monetary Fund, Washington, DC, 7 January (http://www.imf.org/external/np/pp/eng/2011/010711.pdf).

Jacques, Martin (2009). *When China Rules the World: The End of the Western World and the Birth of a New Global Order*, Penguin Books, New York.

Kissinger, Henry (2011). *On China*, Penguin, New York.

Kissinger, Henry (2014). *World Order*, Penguin, New York.

Kobayashi, Takuma (2017). 'Overcapacity in China After Economic Crisis: In Relation to Industrial Location', *The Journal of Comparative Economic Studies*, Vol. 12, December, pp. 143–160.

Kolodko, Grzegorz W. (1986a). 'The Repressed Inflation and Inflationary Overhang under Socialism', Faculty Working Paper, No. 1228, Bureau of Economic and Business Research, University of Illinois, Urbana-Champaign.

Kolodko, Grzegorz W. (1986b). 'Economic Growth Cycles in the Centrally Planned Economies: A Hypothesis of the "Long Cycle"', Faculty Working Paper, No. 1280, Bureau of Economic and Business Research, University of Illinois, Urbana-Champaign.

Kolodko, Grzegorz W. (1999a). 'Equity Issues in Policymaking in Transition Economies', in Vito Tanzi, Ke-young Chu and Sanjeev Gupta (eds.), *Economic Policy and Equity*, International Monetary Fund, Washington, DC, pp. 150–188.

Kolodko, Grzegorz W. (1999b). 'Transition to a Market Economy and Sustained Growth: Implications for the Post-Washington Consensus', *Communist and Post-Communist Studies*, Vol. 32, No. 3, pp. 233–261.

Kolodko, Grzegorz W. (2000a). *From Shock to Therapy: The Political Economy of Postsocialist Transformation*, Oxford University Press, New York.

Kolodko, Grzegorz W. (2000b). *Post-Communist Transition: The Thorny Road*, University of Rochester Press, Rochester, NY.

Kolodko, Grzegorz W. (2002). *Globalization and Catching-up in Transition Economies*, University of Rochester Press, Rochester, NY.

Kolodko, Grzegorz W. (2004). 'Institutions, Policies and Growth', *Rivista di Politica Economica*, May–June, pp. 45–79.

Kolodko, Grzegorz W. (2011a). *Truth, Error and Lies: Politics and Economics in a Volatile World*, Columbia University Press, New York.

Kolodko, Grzegorz W. (2011b) 'New Pragmatism Versus Failing Neoliberalism', *Let's Talk Development* [blog], World Bank Chief Economist, 25 February (https://blogs.worldbank.org/developmenttalk/new-pragmatism-versus-failing-neoliberalism).

Kolodko, Grzegorz W. (2014a). *Whither the World: Political Economy of the Future*, Palgrave Macmillan, New York.

Kolodko, Grzegorz W. (2014b). 'Bring Poland to the G20, and Don't Cry for Argentina', *The Economist*, 1 March.

Kolodko, Grzegorz W. (2014c). 'The New Pragmatism, or Economics and Policy for the Future', *Acta Oeconomica*, Vol. 64, No. 2, pp. 139–160.

Kolodko, Grzegorz W. (2014d). 'Cold War II', *Blog – Volatile World* [blog], post 2506, 10 November (http://www.wedrujacyswiat.pl/blog/gwk_BLOG.pdf).

Kolodko, Grzegorz W. (2016). 'How to Destroy a Country. The Economics and the Politics of the Greek Crisis', *Rivista di Politica Economica*, No. IV–VI (April/June), pp. 37–61.

Kolodko, Grzegorz W. (2017). 'Will China Save the World?', Roubini EconoMonitor, 24 May (http://www.economonitor.com/blog/2017/05/will-china-save-the-world/).

Kolodko, Grzegorz W. and Walter W. McMahon (1987). 'Stagflation and Shortageflation: A Comparative Approach', *Kyklos*, Vol. 40, No. 2, pp. 176–197 (http://www.tiger.edu.pl/kolodko/artykuly/Stagflation_and_Shortageflation.pdf).

Kolodko, Grzegorz W. and Mario D. Nuti (1997). 'The Polish Alternative: Old Myths, Hard Facts and New Strategies in the Successful Transformation of the Polish Economy', *Research for Action*, No. 33, United Nations University World Institute for Development Economics.

Kornai, János (1971). *Anti-Equilibrium: On Economic System Theory and the Task of Research*, North Holland Publishing Co., Amsterdam.

Kornai, János (1980). *Economics of Shortage*, North Holland Publishing Co., Amsterdam.

Kornai, János (1986). 'The Soft Budget Constraints', *Kyklos*, Vol. 39, No. 1, pp. 3–30.

Kornai, János (1990). *The Road to a Free Economy: Shifting from a Socialist System. The Example of Hungary*, W. W. Norton and Company, London.

Kornai, János (1992). *The Socialist System: The Political Economy of Communism*, Princeton University Press, Princeton, NJ.

Kornai, János (2014). *Dynamism, Rivalry, and the Surplus Economy. Two Essays on the Nature of Capitalism*, Oxford University Press, Oxford.

Kornai, János and Yingyi Qian (2009). *Market and Socialism: In the Light of the Experiences of China and Vietnam*, Palgrave Macmillan, Basingstoke.

Kraemer, Kenneth L., Greg Linden and Jason Dedrick (2011). 'Capturing Value in Global Networks: Apple's iPad and iPhone', PCIC Working Paper, Personal Computing Industry Center, University of California, Irvine, July (http://pcic.merage.uci.edu/papers/2011/value_ipad_iphone.pdf).

Kupchan, Charles A. (2012). *No One's World: The West, the Rising Rest, and the Coming Global Turn*, Oxford University Press, New York.

Lange, Oskar (1963). *Political Economy. Volume 1: General Problems*, Pergamon Press, Oxford.

Lange, Oskar (1971). *Political Economy. Volume 2*, Pergamon Press, Oxford; PWN – Polish Scientific Publisher, Warsaw.

Lardy, Nicholas R. (2014). *Markets Over Mao: The Rise of Private Business in China*, Peterson Institute of International Economies, Washington, DC.

Lin, Justin Yifu (2004). 'Lessons of China's Transition from a Planned Economy to a Market Economy', Distinguished Lectures Series, No. 16, Leon Kozminski Academy of Entrepreneurship and Management, Warsaw (www.tiger.edu.pl/publikacje/dist/lin.pdf).

Lin, Justin Yifu (2012a). *Demystifying the Chinese Economy*, Cambridge University Press, Cambridge.

Lin, Justin Yifu (2012b). *New Structural Economics: A Framework for Rethinking Development and Policy*, The World Bank, Washington, DC.

Marcus, Jonathan (2018). 'The "Globalisation" of China's Military Power', BBC News, 13 February (http://www.bbc.com/news/world-asia-china-43036302).

Marx, Karl (1992). *Capital: Volume 1: A Critique of Political Economy*, Penguin Classics, London.

Marx, Karl and Friedrich Engels (2014). *The Communist Manifesto*, International Publishers, New York.

Matthew, Oliver (2017). 'Chinese Outbound Tourists – New 2017 Report', 'Thematic Report', CLSA, Hong Kong, 17 July (https://www.clsa.com/idea/chinese-tourists-expand-their-horizons/).

McGregor, James (2012). *No Ancient Wisdom, No Followers: The Challenges of Chinese Authoritarian Capitalism*, Prospecta Press, Westport, CT.

Milanovic, Branko (2016). *Global Inequality for the Age of Globalization*, The Belknap Press of Harvard University Press, Cambridge, MA.

Minxin, Pei (2016). *China's Crony Capitalism: The Dynamics of Regime Decay*, Harvard University Press, Cambridge, MA.

Moody, Andrew (2017). 'Prescient Author Now Rules the Roost', *China Daily*, 17 November, p. 20.

Morris, Ian (2010). *Why the West Rules – for Now: The Patterns of History and What They Reveal About the Future*, Profile Books, London.

Mosher, Steven W. (2017). *Bully of China: Why China's Dream Is the New Threat to World Order*, Regnery Publishing, Washington, DC.

Naughton, Barry (2017). 'Is China Socialist?', *Journal of Economic Perspectives*, Vol. 31, No. 1, pp. 3–24.

Naughton, Barry and Kellee S. Tsai (eds.) (2015). *State Capitalism, Institutional Adaptation, and the Chinese Miracle*, Cambridge University Press, New York.

New York Times (2017). 'A Historic Tax Heist', *The New York Times*, 2 December (https://www.nytimes.com/2017/12/02/opinion/editorials/a-historic-tax-heist.html).

North, Douglass C. (1990). *Institutions, Institutional Change and Economic Performance*, Cambridge University Press, New York.

North, Douglass C. (2005). *Understanding the Process of Economic Change*, Princeton University Press, Princeton, NJ.

Nuti, Domenico Mario (1986). 'Hidden and Repressed Inflation in Soviet-Type Economies: Definitions, Measurements and Stabilization', *Contributions to Political Economy*, Vol. 5, No. 1, pp. 37–82.

Nuti, D. Mario (2018a). 'Kornai: Shortage Versus Surplus Economies', *Acta Oeconomica*, Vol. 68, No. 1, pp. 85–98.

Nuti, D. Mario (2018b). *The Rise and Fall of Socialism*, DOC-RI, Berlin (https://doc-research.org/wp-content/uploads/2019/01/The-rise-and-fall-of-socialism_Download-file.pdf).

OECD (2005). *OECD Economic Surveys: China*, Vol. 13, Organization for Economic Co-operation and Development, Paris (http://homepage.ntu.edu.tw/~lbh/ref/OECD/42.pdf).

O'Neill, Jim (2012). *The Growth Map. Economic Opportunity in the BRICs and Beyond*, Portfolio/Penguin, London.

Ormerod, Paul (1997). *The Death of Economics*, John Wiley & Sons, Inc., New York.

Oxfam (2017). 'An Economy for the 99%', Oxfam Briefing Paper, *Oxfam International*, January (https://www.oxfam.org/en/research/economy-99).

Oxfam (2018). 'Richest 1 Percent Bagged 82 Percent of Wealth Created Last Year – Poorest Half of Humanity Got Nothing', *Oxfam International*, 22 January (https://www.oxfam.org/en/research/economy-99).

Pankaj, Mishra (2012). *From the Ruins of Empire: The Revolt Against the West and the Remaking of Asia*, Farrar, Straus and Giroux, New York.

Parekh, Bhikhu (2013). 'Is Islam a Threat to Europe's Multicultural Democracies?', in Krzysztof Michalski (ed.), *Religion in the New Europe*, Central European University Press, Budapest, pp. 111–121.

Peto, Sandor (2017). 'Hungary Launches Rail Link Tender as CEE-China Summit Starts', Reuters, 26 November (https://www.reuters.com/article/china-hungary-easteurope/hungary-launches-rail-link-tender-as-cee-china-summit-starts-idUSL8N1NW0IC).

Phelps, Edmund S. (2013). *Mass Flourishing: How Grassroots Innovation Created Jobs, Challenge, and Change*, Princeton University Press, New York.

Phelps, Edmund S. (2018). 'Economic Policymaking in the Age of Trump', 'Project Syndicate, 26 January (https://www.project-syndicate.org/onpoint/economic-policymaking-in-the-age-of-trump-by-edmund-s--phelps-2018-01?barrier=accesspaylog).

Piketty, Thomas (2014). *Capital in the Twenty-First Century*, The Belknap Press of Harvard University Press, Cambridge, MA.

Pinker, Steven (2018). *Enlightenment Now: The Case for Reason, Science, Humanism, and Progress*, Viking, New York.

Randers, Jorgen (2012). *2052: A Global Forecast for the Next Forty Years*, Chelsea Green Publishing, White River Junction, VT.

Ridley, Matt (2010). *The Rational Optimist: How Prosperity Evolves*, HarperCollins, New York.

Ringen, Stein (2016). *The Perfect Dictatorship: China in the 21st Century*, Hong Kong University Press, Hong Kong.

Rodrik, Dani (2015). *Economics Rules: Why Economics Works, When It Fails, and How to Tell the Difference*, Oxford University Press, Oxford.

Roubini, Nouriel and Stephen Mihm (2010). *Crisis Economics. A Crash Course in the Future of Finance*, Penguin, New York.

Saunders, Doug (2012). *The Myth of the Muslim Tide: Do Immigrants Threaten the West?*, Vintage Books, New York.

Shambaugh, David (2016). *China's Future*, Polity Press, Cambridge.

Stedman Jones, Gareth (2016). *Karl Marx: Greatness and Illusion*, Allen Lane, Cambridge, MA.

Stiglitz, Joseph E. (1998). 'More Instruments and Broader Goals: Moving Toward the Post-Washington Consensus', WIDER Annual Lecture, 2, UNU-WIDER, Helsinki (https://www.wider.unu.edu/sites/default/files/AL02-1998.pdf).

Stiglitz, Joseph E. (2007). *Making Globalization Work*, W. W. Norton & Company, New York.

Subramanian, and Martin Kessler (2012). 'The Renminbi Bloc Is Here: Asia Down, Rest of the World to Go?', Working Paper, 12–19, Peterson Institute for International Economics, Washington, DC.

Tian, Nan, Aude Fleurant, Peter D. Wezeman and Siemon T. Wezeman (2017). 'Trends in World Military Expenditure, 2016', SIPRI Fact Sheet, Stockholm International Peace Research Institute, April (https://www.sipri.org/sites/default/files/Trends-world-military-expenditure-2016.pdf).

Tinbergen, Jan (1956). *Economic Policy: Principles and Design*, North Holland Publishing Co., Amsterdam.

Tirole, Jean (2017). *Economics of the Common Good*, Princeton University Press, Princeton, NJ.

Tooze, Adam (2007). *The Wages of Destruction: The Making and Breaking of the Nazi Economy*, Viking Penguin, New York.

Townson, Nigel (ed.) (2007). *Spain Transformed: The Franco Dictatorship, 1959–1975*, Palgrave Macmillan, New York.

Vogel, Ezra (2013). *Deng Xiaoping and the Transformation of China*, The Belknap Press of Harvard University Press, Cambridge, MA.

Walicki, Andrzej (1995). *Marxism and the Leap to the Kingdom of Freedom: The Rise and Fall of the Communist Utopia*, Stanford University Press, Stanford, CT.

Watkins, Eli and Abby Phillip (2018). 'Trump Decries Immigrants from "Shithole Countries" Coming to US', CNN, 12 January (https://edition.cnn.com/2018/01/11/politics/immigrants-shithole-countries-trump/index.html).

Wheen, Francis (2004). *How Mumbo Jumbo Conquered the World: A Short History of Modern Delusions*, Public Affairs, New York.

Williamson, John (1990). 'What Washington Means by Policy Reform', in John Williamson (ed.), *Latin American Adjustment: How Much Has Happened?*, Institute for International Economics, Washington, DC, pp. 7–20.

World Bank (1993). *The East Asian Economic Miracle: Economic Growth and Public Policy*, The World Bank, Washington, DC (http://documents. worldbank.org/curated/en/975081468244550798/pdf/multi-page.pdf).

Xi Jinping (2014). *The Governance of China*, Foreign Languages Press, Beijing.

Xi Jinping (2017). 'China's Socialist Democracy the Most Effective', President Xi's report at the 19th Party Congress, Xinhua, 18 October.

Xinzhen, Lan (2017). 'Setting the Course', *China Today*, November, pp. 22–25.

Yi, Yang (2013). 'Youth urged to contribute to realization of "Chinese dream"', Xinhuanet, 4 May.

Zhang, Hui (2017). 'The 19th CPC National Congress Draws Blueprint for National Development', *China Today*, November, pp. 18–21.

Zuckoff, Mitchell (2006). Ponzi's Scheme: The True Story of a Financial Legend, Random House, New York.

Zurcher, Anthony (2018). 'Seven things Trump's $500bn spending splurge tells us', BBC News, 9 February (http://www.bbc.com/news/world-us-canada-43008311).

Index

Africa 13, 32–4, 39–40, 51–2, 55–9, 80, 159
aging population 52, 59, 160
aid programmes 6, 38
Albania 91–2, 151
American dream, the 87
Americanization 85
Ant Financial (company) 22–3
anti-access area denial (A2AD) 8
Apple (company) 31, 76
Arab Spring 13, 111, 151
arms race 8
art works 84
artificial intelligence (AI) 60
Asia 27–53, 55–9, 61–6, 70, 73–8, 80–3, 86–7
leading role of China in 27
Asian Development Bank (ADB) 39
'Asian economic miracle' 65
Asian Infrastructure Investment Bank (AIIB) 80–1
Association of South East Asian Nations (ASEAN) 29
Australia 36, 40, 48, 67, 74, 80

balance: current 161; ecological 143, 160; environmental 159
Bangladesh 13, 29, 31, 35, 63
'Beijing Consensus' 84–5
Belgrade–Budapest railway 156
Belt and Road Initiative (BRI) 32–6, 157; *see also* New Silk Road programme
birth control 59
'black or white cat' strategy 132, 143
Brazil 13, 48–9
'BRIC' countries 48, 80
Broadcom (company) 22
budget constraints, *hard* and *soft* 108–10, 122

budget deficits 149; financed by China 137–9
Bush, George (senior) 22

Canada 23, 79, 159
capital 3, 14–16, 25, 28, 32, 36–9, 49, 68, 76–7, 90, 98, 118, 133–4, 137, 142, 146, 151, 156
capitalism 16, 76–8, 83–9 *passim*; definition of 90; *European* and *Asian* types of 77
central and eastern Europe (CEE) 32–5, 44–51, 89, 95–100, 109, 133–4, 142–5, 151–6
centrally-planned economies 15, 99–100, 158
Chávez, Hugo 98
Chengdu 118
China 3–17, 21–52, 109–17, 123, 141–7; capital markets in 49; constitution of 128–9; demographic trends 52, 55–7, 60–2; foreign direct investment from 51; market values of companies 49; the middle class in 89; other countries' opinions about 157–8; research centers in 142; role in Asia and in the world 27, 156–7, 164; shortages in 109–10; slow-down in economic growth 41; state control of the economy 133; students in 39, 146–7; suspicion of 38, 150; trading partners of 40; Twelfth Five-Year Plan (2013) 68; use of financial reserves 137–40, 151
'Chinese characteristics' 121–9
Chinese Communist Party 114, 128–9
'Chinese spirit' 39

'Chinism' 89–132, 133
Christianity 59
clash of civilizations 76, 86
climate change 150
coexistence, peaceful 83, 129
Cold War One 5–6, 20, 25, 82, 95,
    129, 156
Cold War Two 5–6
communism 12, 94–8; *see also*
    Chinese Communist Party
competitiveness 31
Confucius 86, 131
consumers' markets 101–2
convergence of systems 130–1
corruption 127
Credit Lyonnais Securities Asia
    (CLSA) 75
crisis 41, 47–8, 51, 58, 69, 76, 78, 83,
    98, 111, 133–6, 139, 145
crony capitalism 112, 128
crossroads of history 1
Czech Republic 50, 154

debt problems 137–9
demand 50, 62, 65, 72, 100–3, 106–9
demand for money 108
'democracy index' 121–2
democratic processes 110–11
'demographic dividend' 29, 60, 64
demographic processes 52, 55–7,
    60–2, 164
Deng Xiaoping 103, 116, 126, 132–3
dependency ratio 62–3
deregulation of the economy 134
détente 83
developmental states 123
Dickens, Charles 130
distribution of income and wealth 1,
    18–19, 50, 134–5, 160, 164
Doomsday Clock 19–20
Duda, Andrzej 37

eastern Europe *see* central and
    eastern Europe
The Economist 8–9
Economist Intelligence Unit 121

Eichengreen, Barry 66
emancipating 6, 38–41, 73–4, 77–80,
    85
emancipating economies 6, 39, 41,
    73–4, 77–80, 85
emerging markets 48, 87, 97
'end of history' doctrine 129
Engels, Friedrich 95
enlightened authoritarianism 111–12
entrepreneurial middle class 89
environmental issues 1, 16, 72,
    159–60
equilibrium 16, 99–101, 106–9, 163
European Union (EU) 13, 21, 25, 35,
    42, 44, 89, 155
existential rationality 1–2, 163–4

family planning *see* birth control
fertility replacement rate 57
Finland 35–6
First World War 5
forecasts: demographic 57–8, 63–4;
    unreliability of 48
forced money savings 104
foreign direct investment (FDI) 51,
    151–2
foreign exchange reserves 150
Fortune "Global 500" companies 125
Fourier, Charles 98
France 8, 13, 17, 30, 37, 75, 77, 98, 124
Franco, Francisco 112
free trade and free market ideology
    24, 87
Freeman, Chas 131
Friedman, Milton 126
'from each according to his ability,
    and to each according to his
    need' 94
Fukuyama, Francis 129
future 1–4, 15–16, 27–32, 58, 62–6,
    76–7, 86–7, 111–12, 125–31, 139,
    145, 149–50, 157–61, 165

Galbraith, James K. 78, 91
geopolitics 20, 42, 58, 73, 80, 87, 144,
    154–5

Germany 12–13, 17, 38, 40, 48–9,
 58–9, 92, 95, 97, 112, 124
global financial and economic crisis
 (2008) 76, 111
globalization 2–5, 18, 25–6, 28, 30,
 33, 37, 60, 124, 135, 142, 149, 159,
 163–4
Goldman Sachs (investment bank) 48
Greece 13, 35–6, 156
gross domestic product (GDP) 7, 45,
 66–8, 80, 135
growth models, economic 70–1
growth rates 41–7, 50
G7 group 78
G20 group 79–80

'hard landing' 47–8, 50
Hegel, G.W.F. 129
heterodoxy 87
Hitler, Adolf 112
Hollande, François 98
Huang, Yukon 128
Huawei (company) 22, 24, 76
human capital 14–15, 37, 137, 146
Hungary 70, 91–2, 94, 97, 102–4

imitation strategy 71
imperialism 12, 51
inclusive 5, 33, 124, 149, 159, 163
inclusive globalization 124
income thresholds for GDP and
 growth 66–8
India 29, 41–8, 55, 57, 76–7
industrial policy 9
inequality *see* distribution of income
 and wealth
inflation 94, 104–8
infrastructure projects 140, 152, 156
institutionalizing international
 economic cooperation 155
institutions 2, 14–16, 69, 81, 86, 90,
 111, 121, 128, 155
intellectual property violations 120
International Monetary Fund (IMF)
 21, 39, 48

investment 16, 20, 31–7, 48, 51, 60,
 68, 72, 75–6, 80, 94, 99, 114–15,
 130, 137–40, 143, 151
Iran nuclear deal 17
Iraq 18, 38
Islam 59

Jacques, Martin 128
Japan 29, 35, 40, 48, 59–60, 67, 74

Keynesian policies 3
Kissinger, Henry 130–1
Korea *see* North Korea; South Korea
Kornai, János 96, 100, 104, 106
Kosovo 152–5

Latin America 13, 32, 36, 84, 98
Lenovo (company) 24
Leonardo da Vinci 84
Li Keqiang 155
Lin, Justin Yifu 126–8
long-term thinking 130–1

McCarthy, Joseph 11
macroeconomic stabilization state 123
Macron, Emmanuel 37, 98, 150
Maduro, Nicolás 98–9
Mao Zedong 32–3, 130
market economies 14, 164
market mechanisms 2, 120–3, 130
Marx, Karl 95, 99, 113
May, Theresa 37
Mediterranean culture 73
Merkel, Angela 12
Mexico 11, 36, 57
Middle East 17, 61
middle-income trap 68, 71, 126
migration 18, 58, 60, 63, 116
military spending 6–7
money market 43
monopoly 99
Moody, Andrew 128
Motorola (company) 76
Mugabe, Robert 98
Mujica, José 'Pepe' 99

multiculturalism 87
multipolarity 86

nationalism 18, 58, 77, 133, 159;
    economic 149
natural rate of unemployment 106
Naughton, Barry 93
neoliberalism 18, 76, 78, 86, 123,
    133–9, 149, 159
new nationalism 18, 58, 77, 81, 133,
    159
new pragmatism 86, 91, 126–8, 133,
    143, 158–9
New Silk Road programme 32–3,
    36–40, 120, 124, 152
Niger 57
Nigeria 14, 30, 55–6, 69
'19+1' initiative 154
Nixon, Richard 82–3, 130
Nokia (company) 76
North Korea 9, 17, 23, 35
nuclear weapons 17
Nuti, Mario D. 93–4

Obama, Barack 22
one-child policy 61–2
outsourcing of business activities 31–2
Owen, Robert 98

Papua New Guinea 35–6
Paris climate accord (2015) 17, 150,
    159
Park, Chung-hee 112
Park, Donghyun 66
Pax Romana, Pax Americana and *Pax
    Sinica* 164
people: retirement-age 52, 60, 62;
    working-age 52, 61–4; young 59,
    62, 158
the Philippines 35
Phillips curve 105
Pinochet, Augusto 112
Poland 11, 20, 26, 37, 48, 50, 62, 102,
    122, 126–7, 141–4, 151–3
Pompeo, Mike 11

Ponzi scheme 116
population 1, 15–19, 27–9, 33, 42–5,
    51–2, 55–65, 71–2, 75, 79–82, 90,
    93, 99–100, 103, 107, 112, 118–20,
    140, 146, 151–2, 160; of the
    world 1; by region 57
populism 133, 136
'post-communist' and 'post-socialist'
    countries 96
price controls 103–4
price of money 170
privatization of state assets 114
producers' markets 101–2
profits' share of GDP 135
property relations 113–16
protectionism 1, 10–11, 20–5, 30, 36
public goods state 123
purchasing power parity (PPP) 42–3
Putin, Vladimir 6

Qatar 61
Qi Baishi 84

Reagan, Ronald 134–5
regulation of the economy 2, 16, 85,
    134
reinstitutionalizing globalization 80,
    124
remittances 61
renminbi currency 83–4
Revolution: Communist 33; French
    130; Industrial 28; Technological
    135
robotics 64
Romney, Mitt 22
rule of law 24
Russia 5–8, 11, 18, 37, 46, 61

Saint-Simon, Henri de 98
Salvador 36
Samsung (company) 24, 76
sanctions, economic 25
Sanders, Bernie 98
Sany Group Co. 22
saving, propensity for 151

savings 16, 104
Scandinavian countries 95, 159
Shanghai 32, 118, 142, 150
Shanghai Cooperation Organization (SCO) 81–2
Shanxinhui swindle (2016–2017) 116
Shin, Kwanho 66
shortageflation (SHF) 104, 107, 109–10
shortages 99–110, 122
short-termism 12–13
'Sinodependency index'40–1
Sinophobia 8–9
'16+1' initiative 152, 155, 157
social exclusion 135
social market economies 112, 127, 164
socialism 89–100, 103–9, 112–14, 118–31; constitutive elements of 93–4; four criteria for 93
Socialism with Chinese characteristics 94, 121, 127
'soft landing' 47–8, 72
soft loans 110
South Africa 13
South Asian Association for Regional Cooperation (SAARC) 29
South Korea 13, 35, 40, 67, 112
Soviet Union 15, 37, 42, 109, 133–4
stagflation (SF) 104–5
Stalinism 96
standard of living 65, 107
state capitalism 78, 94, 98, 112–13, 123, 125
state-owned enterprises (SOEs) 65, 77, 110, 114–18, 124–5
state socialism 15
supply 29, 32, 34, 51, 60, 62, 65, 91, 100–1, 106–9
supply of money 108
surpluses, economies of 101–2
Switzerland 38
Syria 18
Szijjarto, Peter 155–6

Taiwan 40
taxation changes 136–9

technological change 70
terms in office, limits on 2
terrorism 18, 28, 38
think tanks 142
Tillerson, Rex 51
total fertility rate (TFR) 57
tourism 74–5
trade wars 20–3
Trans-Pacific Partnership (TPP) 80–1
triple balance 143
Trump, Donald 8, 10, 17, 20–2, 36, 52, 82–3, 135–6, 149–50, 163
'Trumponomics' 149

Ukraine 18, 46, 50, 154
unemployment 98, 105–7, 109, 137
United Kingdom 8, 37, 67
United Nations (UN) Organization 55, 58
United States (US) 5–11, 20–6, 31, 35, 42, 44, 51–2, 67, 111, 134–9, 149, 156, 163; Federal Reserve 138; House of Representatives 136
urbanization 69
utopian socialists 98

Vietnam 29, 35, 63, 78, 81, 92, 97, 109

Wang Yi 36
warfare 5
'Washington Consensus' 84–5, 125
the West 1, 37, 74–6
westernization 85
win-win globalization 124
working-age population 62–4
World Bank 39
World Trade Organization (WTO) 21, 25, 120, 122

Xi Jinping 12, 37, 87–8, 125–9, 149–50

young people's views 158

Zhou Enlai 130–1
Zimbabwe 98
ZTE Corporation 23–4, 76